The Napoleonic Wars

One Shot at Glory1803-1815

The Napoleonic Wars: One Shot at Glory

Great Wars of the World

History Nerds

Published by History Nerds, 2020.

THE NAPOLEONIC WARS: ONE SHOT AT GLORY

First edition. December 23, 2020.

Copyright © 2020 History Nerds.

ISBN: 979-8215451281

Written by History Nerds.

Also by History Nerds

Celtic History
Ireland

Great Wars of the World
World War 1
World War 2
The Napoleonic Wars: One Shot at Glory
The Serbian Revolution: 1804-1835
Peace Won by the Saber: The Crimean War, 1853-1856
The Wars of the Roses

Irish Heroes
Grace O'Malley: The Pirate Queen of Ireland
William Butler Yeats: Nobel Prize Winning Poet
Scáthach
Finn McCool

The History of the Vikings

Vikings
Longships on Restless Seas

The Rise and Fall of Empires
Rome: The Rise and Fall

Standalone
The History of the United Kingdom
The History of Ireland
The History of America
Stalin
The Fiery Maelstrom of Freedom
The History of Scotland
Robert the Bruce
William Wallace: Scotland's Great Freedom Fighter
The History of Wales

Table of Contents

Introduction

THE FRENCH REVOLUTION of the late 1790's was one of the critical events in the history of Europe. It was the defining moment – a historic landslide that ushered the world into a new, completely different epoch. Alas, all such changes come at a great cost. In the wake of the Revolution, a series of large scale conflicts ensued, which are collectively known as the Napoleonic Wars. Their magnitude, their ferocity, and the loss of lives they caused were unprecedented up to that time, and shown to the observing world that the changing of a thousand year old history can be brutal, vicious, and tumultuous.

By the early 1800's it was becoming clear that the Napoleonic Wars were unlike anything the World experienced: In many ways, these conflicts surpassed the *Thirty Years' War* of the mid 1600's. They were the wars of grand scale, of tactics and strategy. Wars of boldness and gamble – of generals and emperors. These wars were the final, blazing spark of a rapidly changing Europe – the last conflict before the coming of a new age: of industry, fall of monarchy, and the World Wars. Nevertheless, they left a significant mark on the world as we know it, setting the stage for greater things yet to come – erasing generations in the process.

And as is the case with every large scale, global conflict, the Napoleonic Wars was the inevitable result of a powerful ruler's rise to power – and his yearning for more and more. Napoleon Bonaparte was the ruler in question here. Idolized by many, and despised by even more, Napoleon cast his shadow over much of Europe, establishing a short but decisive French dominion over the continent.

Bonaparte was born in Corsica, in a family of minor Italian nobility that originated in Tuscany. A deft gambler and opportunist, Napoleon rose through the military ranks, driven by a thirst for power and influence. He came to power in the wake of the French Revolution and established a military dictatorship in the already unstable, chaotic nation. Yet even so, he managed to reinstate stability, to revive its finances and establish a dependent bureaucracy, and to raise a powerful army – all of it in a short amount of time. His skill and daring made him revered and respected by some. But the devastation into which he plunged Europe made him hated by most. The story of the Napoleonic Wars is the story of Europe's tragedy: of brother-wars and of blood shed in vain. It is as much a Napoleon's story as it is the story of millions of men that died because of him. Join us as we embark on a dramatic journey of a bygone era, a journey through gunpowder smoke and glorious cavalry charges!

Chapter I
The Giant's Rise
Background and Prelude to the
Napoleonic Wars

THE FRENCH REVOLUTION was undoubtedly the most critical event that preceded the rise of the Napoleonic Wars. This period shook Europe in a way that was not seen and felt for over a century, and laid the tables for a struggle to surpass all that came before it. From around 1787, Europe experienced a complex and widespread political and socio-economic struggle, and the French Revolution played the key role within it. Contemporary to the Revolution, a series of diplomatic alliances and shifting levels of power among major European states brought a rapid deterioration between the key powers and drove the continent towards a looming conflict. Austria and Prussia reached a surprising diplomatic alliance; and In the East, Russia was growing increasingly powerful, and continued its steady expansion. However, that expansion caused growing disapproval from Russia's two major neighbors - Turkey and Poland, at whose expense the expansion proceeded. This escalated into the Russo-Turkish War of 1787, a conflict that dragged on until 1792 - all into the favor of Russia. In fact, the Ottoman Turks and the Russians led a series of wars before: this time, the Ottomans began a conflict in order to regain the territories lost to the Russians. Their attempt was an eventual failure, and only served to strengthen Russia, solidify its borders, and give it a strong position on the Black Sea.

On the other side, Russia experienced growing tensions with Poland - with whom, again, they had a lengthy history of discontent. The Polish King and Grand Duke of Lithuania, Stanisław August Poniatowski (Stanislaus II Augustus), was in the rapid process of strengthening the Polish state with the means of a series of reforms. Doing so, he was acting against the wishes and aims of Russia's Empress Catherine the Great, whose lover he once was. Also, it is she that helped bring Poniatowski to the Polish throne in the first place. Nevertheless, the growing power and independence of Poland was seen as a potential hindrance for the Russian expansion and power. Poniatowski knew that he will need allies in order to remain on that steady, rising course, and looked towards his traditional ally - France. However, the French Revolution was beginning in 1792, and Poland could in no way rely on France's help. Thus, in 1792, contributing to the overall rising chaos in Europe, Russia invaded Poland leading to the Polish-Russian War of 1792, which lasted roughly 2 months and led to the Second Partition of Poland in 1793, through which it lost a lot of territories. By 1795 and the Third Partition, the Polish-Lithuanian Commonwealth ceased to exist, as did the sovereign states of Poland and Lithuania. Of course, all of this meant that Russia gained a lot more territory and power.

In the west though, in France, things were looking increasingly dire. The French Monarchy, the so-called *Ancien Régime* (Old Regime), was both the political and social regime in France for several centuries up to that point, but it began to fail in several key points. By 1780's, the Old Regime grew immensely unpopular amongst the common French folk, and was even openly hated. France at that time was suffering from a series of economic difficulties, even if it was one of the richest European nations. However, the wealth was not for all: most of it was reserved for the nobility and the court of the French monarchy. The biggest factors of this period of instability was social inequality, and taxation. This meant that both the low, peasant class, and the middle and upper class *bourgeoisie,* were all faced with extremely high taxes, most of which went to the unimaginably rich noble, who thus kept up their lavish and hedonistic lifestyles.

Thus, year by year, tax by tax, the aristocrats and the court of the Old Regime was growing unpopular, and faced the majority of the French nation as its rising opponent. A gradual change in the French society clearly separated these social classes: the ambitious and successful middle class merchants, farmers, and traders, alongside the aggrieved peasants, workers, and scholars, all faced the same plight and the same oppression from the nobility. Also, the rise of the French and other European philosophers, many of whom presented ideas of Enlightenment, social theory, equality, and freedom of the individual, gave a new viewpoint to the common man, a new and growing sense of freedom that was taken from him.

And when France was unable to effectively finance its government debt, an economic depression ensued, bringing with it high food prices, widespread unemployment, and an emerging crisis that the French King Louis XVI could not contain.

Louis XVI was thus becoming increasingly inept and hated. On the political scene, he continuously refused to rule as a *constitutional* monarch, i.e. exercising authority in accordance to a written (or unwritten) constitution. He kept to his rule as an *absolute* monarch, continuing that form of rule in France for over a thousand years.

The discontent of the French people spilled over in 1789, marking the beginning of the French Revolution, and a period of chaos in France that would last for roughly 10 years. One of the iconic events from the fated 1789 is the *Storming of Bastille*, which perfectly showcased the rise of the chaos and the extent of the anger of the French folk. The fall of the royal fortress of the Bastille before the enraged masses was seen as an enormous and symbolic victory. *Bastille Day* is celebrated even today.

By September 1792, the Old Regime was abolished after several centuries of rule over France. On September 22nd, 1792, the First

French Republic was declared, and in 1793, Louis XVI was executed on the guillotine. His death was seen as a historic, turning point in both the history of France and of Europe. However, all of this chaotic unrest in France saw the rise of one powerful individual - Napoleon.

Born in 1769 in Corsica, into a family of minor Corsican nobility that had origins in central Italy, Napoleon Bonaparte rose through the ranks of the army and used the French Revolution as a veritable ladder towards power. From his family in Corsica, he embarked onto a military career, studying and training at the Military Academy in Brienne, and subsequently in the Military School in Paris, where he gained a commission in the artillery by 1785. During his youth, he was inspired by the contemporary philosophies of enlightenment, patriotism, and socio-political reform. He also drew great inspiration and identified with Alexander the Great. Many historians describe Napoleon as an *outsider* figure, a person who was often on the margins of the French society, with a penchant for violence, frustration, and domination. Born as a fourth child and a third son, he possibly gained these traits due to the competition with his siblings, and a strict upbringing.

His character was also marked - perhaps most importantly - by immense opportunism. When he came to the rule, Napoleon would not hesitate to satisfy his immense drive for power on the expense of his family - if they failed to serve his interests and political power.

Young Napoleon graduated in 1785, and this marks his rapid and steady advance towards power. Led by his insatiable desire for power and command, he rose through the ranks and acquired command quite early on in his career. Before the beginning of the Revolution in 1789, he served as a second lieutenant in an artillery regiment. However, fueled by his strong Corsican pride and sense of belonging, he harbored strong patriotic pride and thus ended up in Corsica, serving in the conflict that was ongoing there. But as the French Revolution progressed, he too shifted his focus towards mainland France and the affairs there.

By 1792, he was promoted a Captain in the French army, commanding over a battalion of volunteer troops, as the period of European conflicts, known as the French Revolutionary Wars, was beginning. In these conflicts, Napoleon gained control over the French *Army of Italy*, commanding over it in the Campaigns in Italy. His prowess as a military commander and a strategist was quickly recognized in this campaign, where he managed to knock out the Piedmont army out of the conflict in just two weeks, after a series of dazzling victories.

During the French Revolutionary Wars, and the Italian Campaign in particular, Napoleon greatly honed his skill for the future conflicts. He relied on new and bold military tactics, and employed a never before seen set of strategies. Napoleon, as a graduate of military schools, skillfully applied the conventional ideas to dynamic real world situations. One of his trademark approaches to combat was the use of artillery in a highly mobile role, which was employed in support of his infantry. He also relied on skilled concealment of his own deployment of troops on the battlefield, and an emphasis on envelopment of the enemy force.

For France, the Italian Campaign in the Revolutionary Wars was a great success, but it was also very important as a stepping stone for Napoleon. During this period, he became a highly influential figure in French politics, and got the chance to use his propaganda and manipulation skills, which were a big part of his opportunist personality.

And it is during the campaign in Italy that we can finally get a glimpse of the true nature of Napoleon's rise to power and his insatiable drive: during the operations, he "looted" an enormous amount of funds from Italy - an estimated $45 million in funds, and a further $12 million in precious metals and jewels. Back in France's political spheres, his opponents accused him of dictatorial pretensions. All the while, Napoleon circulated his propaganda newspapers both in France and amongst his troops in the field.

In many regards, Napoleon's rise was dazzlingly fast. Following the bold coup d'etat, known as the Coup de 18 Brumaire, Napoleon seized power in France and established a Consulate, himself being the First Consul. This action was the de-facto turning point of his rise, essentially making France into a dictatorship. It is important to remember that when Napoleon came to power in France, it was a nation in great disorder, following the events of the French Revolution. Nevertheless, he managed to reorganize its army, to stabilize the economy, and create a stable nation once more. His emphasis on a reorganized and strengthened army was clear, and soon enough France boasted great numbers of men and reserves.

Following the so-called *Treaty of Amiens* of the French Revolutionary Wars, tensions between Britain and France continued to be at an all-time high. Bold and decisive, opportunist Napoleon had annexed the Italian regions of Elba and Piedmont, and also made himself the President of the Italian Republic, a puppet state created by France. Furthermore, he failed to fulfill several of the aspects in the Treaty of Amiens that were previously established.

One of the main focuses of the deteriorated Anglo-French relations of the period was trade. This was one of the causes for Napoleon's failed Egypt and Syria Expedition of 1798, through which he sought to weaken Britain's trade routes towards India, and also strengthen French trade interests. With the British Navy dealing a crushing defeat at the Battle of Nile, and the defeat at the Battle of Alexandria, Napoleon's short Egyptian campaign ended without success.

Malta was another point of discontent between the two powers. The Treaty of Amiens focused in particular on this island, which was captured by the British in the French Revolutionary Wars. Further destabilization was caused with the French invasion of Switzerland in 1798, with which Napoleon sought to impose central authority over that nation. The traditional Swiss confederation of self-governing cantons was disbanded, and instead Napoleon created an allied (puppet) state of Helvetic Republic. The change was deeply resented in Switzerland, and soon enough violent conflicts broke out throughout the land. The British saw these actions as another violation, and Napoleon's actions in Switzerland caused a widespread outrage.

By early 1803, the tensions between France and England were reaching an all-time high. Russia at the time gave its guarantees for support for the British matter in Malta, while the latter suspected a new French invasion of Egypt. This stemmed from a government paper that was published as a report in France, stating that Egypt can be conquered with ease. Due to this information, the British demanded "satisfaction" and a security from France about their intentions. This was directly related to the British evacuation from Malta, which could be used as a "waystation" and a stepping stone towards Egypt. France denied any intent to seize Egypt.

With the failure of the British to evacuate Malta, and their issuing of an ultimatum to France, tensions were at a critical point. The ultimatum demanded the retention of Malta for at least another ten years, as well as the acquisition of the Lampedusa Island, and the French to evacuate Holland. The British offered to recognize France's gains in Italy, under the condition that they leave Switzerland and compensate the Sardinian King for his territorial losses. In response to this ultimatum, France tried to appease the British: they made an offer to place Malta in Russian hands as to give the British the satisfaction they required, and also to leave Holland once Malta was evacuated. The British falsely denied the Russian offer made previously, and their ambassador hastily left Paris. Napoleon was still invested into avoiding another conflict and war and thus proposed a secret offer to the British, by which he would allow them to remain in Malta in exchange for French occupation of Otranto Peninsula in Naples. The offer was disregarded, and all Napoleon's attempts at avoiding a new war were in vain - On May 18th, 1803, the British declared war on France.

It is important to note at this stage that the exact dates in regards to the French Revolutionary Wars and the Napoleonic Wars are uncertain and debated - there is no exact agreed date where one ended and the other began. Some historians propose that the Napoleonic Wars began on the day when Napoleon seized power as a consul, on November 9th 1799, after the coup d'etat. It is true that the state of war existed for several years prior to what is officially considered the beginning of the Napoleonic Wars. These are known today as the French Revolutionary Wars, the European conflict that emerged as a result of the French Revolution, and have officially lasted from roughly April 20th 1792 to March 27th 1802. It pitted France and its allies against Russia, Prussia, Holy Roman Empire, and Britain, or the so-called First and Second Coalition. However, it is as expansive a subject as are the Napoleonic Wars themselves, and addressing the French Revolutionary Wars in full detail is not possible within the scope of this book.

In these regards, it is worth the mention as it served as a great precursor to an ever greater conflict that followed (Napoleonic Wars) and also as a crucial formative period of Napoleon Bonaparte as a political figure, a leader, military strategist, and a ruler. Thus we conclude the general overview of the background and the preludes to Napoleonic Wars proper, which lasted from May 18th 1803, to November 20th, 1813.

Chapter II
An Ancient Rivalry
The Conflict Between Britain and France

AT THIS POINT, IT IS important to reflect on the state of affairs in Britain during the period. Contemporary to the events unfolding in France between 1793 and 1815, Britain was one of the major enemies of France. The British Navy was a great thorn in Napoleon's side - one which he attempted to pluck out with no success: firstly he could not improve his own naval power to match the British, and secondly, he tasted defeat on the Nile, facing the prowess of the legendary British Admiral, Sir Horatio Nelson.

At the time, Great Britain was amongst the wealthiest of world major powers, and often gave financial subsidies to its allies in Europe. With all these - and many other - factors combined, Britain was instrumental in Napoleon's eventual defeat. Arguably, it was in its prime - being one of the world's largest colonial empires, and boasted a modern military and skilled military commanders as well. Throughout the war, the traditional British nature of a "tough as nails" British soldier and the shrewd minds of its upper class brought to that idealized image of the Georgian Era Britain.

In the sense of worldview and philosophy, Britain greatly differed from France of the era: while the latter was swept up by the radical new philosophies of the Enlightenment Era, the former was still firmly rooted in conservative and traditional views. Politically too, the difference was crucial: Britain remained royalist and conservative, while France was radical Republican.

The Royal British Navy was arguably its most important asset and force in the war and in commerce. Napoleon's rise to power became a threat to British mainland in earnest, and thus they invested a lot of their finances into the Napoleonic Wars. The Royal Navy played a crucial role in this, through their naval blockades of the French ports, as well as their legendary naval victories. In 1803 however, the Kingdom of Great Britain received a "facelift", and became the United Kingdom after absorbing Ireland.

After the French Revolutionary Wars, the period of volatile and unstable "peace" was short, lasting only from roughly 1801 to 1803 when it erupted once more. But 1803 and onwards was a conflict much more serious and far more advanced: it pitted matured, stabilized, and comparably strong major European powers against one another, putting to the test both the common soldier, and the general as well.

It was a war of skill and strategy, of larger-than-life line battles, and daring cavalry charges. But more importantly, it was one of the last conflicts of a dying age - the culminating explosion of the aged gunpowder age. And the Brits were adamant to come out on top.

One crucial way for them to achieve that was, of course - money. Defeating the might of Napoleon was going to take some serious financing, and the ability to maintain a balance of power for a string of years.

To do so, Britain relied on its combined financial and industrial resources, and their ability to mobilize all of them for the war effort. We need to remember the fact that France had almost twice the population of Britain at the time, with some 30 million citizens compared to 16 million in the United Kingdom. Nevertheless, the British managed to offset this number by relying on state subsidies, paying money for Austrian and Russian soldiers. Roughly £1.5 million was paid as subsidy for every 100,000 Russian soldiers in the field.

Simply put, Britain managed to uphold its economic power and a strong national output, focusing heavily on where it was needed -

primarily in military spheres. A huge bulk of its economic output went towards the expansion of the Royal Navy, its foremost advantage. The number of large "ships of the line" was doubled, as was the number of frigates. The number of sailors also erupted - reaching from roughly 15,000 to 133,000 in just a span of eight years. British naval might forever destroyed Napoleon's ideas of naval dominance and invasion of Britain, keeping him in mainland Europe throughout the war.

The subsidies we mentioned were an essential expense from Britain, and were used to keep Austria and Russia afloat and in the war. Here is an interesting cross section of how the British budget looked like in 1814, after the war - roughly £98 million was the total budget number: of it, £10 million was reserved for the Royal Navy, that same amount for Britain's allies, £40 million was left for the army, and £38 million was the interest on the national debt - which ended up to be almost the double of Britain's total GDP, totaling at £679 million. In total, the Napoleonic Wars cost Britain a whopping £831 million. Nevertheless, this, and the national debt, were both supported by thousands of investors, and of course, the taxpayers. Of the latter, one person - or rather, family - was crucial in financing the British war effort. From circa 1813 to 1815, one *Nathan Mayer Rothschild,* a wealthy Jewish banker, single handedly financed the whole of British war effort, organizing the payment of British subsidies to their allies in Europe, as well as the shipment of precious metal bullion to the armies of Duke of Wellington in mainland Europe. At the time, this man was amongst the, if not *the*, wealthiest man on earth, and the richest figure in the Rothschild banking dynasty.

Chapter III
The Fire Starts
The War of the Third Coalition

THE INITIAL CONFLICT of the Napoleonic Wars - and arguably the one with the most significant events - was known as the War of the Third Coalition. Here, we need to remember the preceding French Revolutionary Wars, and the initial First and Second Coalitions. The War of the Third Coalition lasted from 1803 to 1806, and marks the opening phase of the Napoleonic Wars. The so-called Third Coalition was the alliance of the Holy Roman Empire, the United Kingdom, Naples, Sicily, Sweden, and the Russian Empire, against France under Napoleon and several French client states.

Infuriated by Britain's perseverance to go to war, Napoleon again considered strongly invading Great Britain. To do so, he amassed a great army of 180,000 men at Boulougne-sur-Mer, on the French coast. However, as we previously mentioned, he lacked (knowingly) the naval superiority needed to cross the channel unopposed. Thus, he came up with a daring and complex plan with which he would lure the British fleet away from the channel crossings and allow him an unchallenged invasion. The plan relied on attacking and thus threatening British overseas territories in the West Indies, drawing away the attention of the enemy navy. The result of this Napoleon's plan was the famous Battle of Trafalgar.

Battle of Trafalgar

NAPOLEON'S INTENTIONS in the English Channel were clear - leaving the British Isles vulnerable and open to invasion. A part of his plan was to combine the entirety of the weaker French fleet, with the combined vessels of his allies. With such a combined force he had a chance to gain decisive and swift control of the English Channel in a single daring action. But, while that was the theoretical plan, reality often found a way to stand in the way.

As mentioned, the key task of this combined fleet of Napoleon was to set sail towards the Caribbean, where they would join up with the naval force in station there, restock, and return in strength towards mainland Europe. But here is where the first possible flaw appears - the French command. The French Mediterranean fleet at the time was under the command of Vice Admiral Pierre-Charles Villeneuve. Although a strict and thoroughly obedient naval commander amongst Napoleon's forces, he was far from being the most competent one or daring. In comparison to him, the British Royal Navy prided itself on one of the finest naval commanders of his age, the highly acclaimed Vice Admiral Sir Horatio Nelson. In 1805, Nelson was tasked with continuing the naval blockade of the French forces at Touloun. This blockade was loose - Nelson specifically opted for such a relaxed blockade in hopes of drawing forth the French navy into battle and defeating them. The other part of the British fleet was under the command of Lord Cornwallis, and was blockading the port of Brest. Needless to say, both of these naval blockades were keeping Napoleon's plans grounded.

Nevertheless, Admiral Villeneuve managed to achieve his task with just a little bit of risk taking. This occurred when Nelson's ships were broken from their formations and set off course due to particularly bad weather. Using this as an opportunity to break through, Villeneuve set sail with his fleet, rendezvoused with the allied Spanish fleet and continued on his way to the Caribbean as tasked.

When this was completed, he was to follow Napoleon's strict orders - return to the port of Brest. However, when returning from the Caribbean a few months afterwards, Pierre-Charles Villeneuve showed his lack of tactical experience as a commander, making a considerable blunder. Knowing of the British presence near Brest, Villeneuve feared battle and changed his course not towards Brest, but towards the Spanish port at Cadiz.

Lord Admiral Horatio Nelson received the news of the combined Franco-Spanish fleet at Cadiz on September 2nd, 1805, and immediately acted upon it. By 15th of that same month, his flagship, the prized HMS Victory, was ready. All the while, Cornwallis also made an excellent move, detaching some 20 line ships from his formations at Brest and sending them towards Cadiz, in hopes of bolstering Nelson's force. By September 28th, both fleets were in position near Cadiz - all to the horror of Villeneuve.

The comparison of the opposing navies is crucial when studying the Battle of Trafalgar. It shows us that numerical superiority is not the key to victory in certain cases. This was especially true for the Napoleonic era battlefield, where tactical grasp and superior strategy were often crucial for victory, alongside daring choices. In the Battle of Trafalgar, Lord Horatio Nelson commanded over 27 *ships of the line.* This term denotes a standard *warship* of the era. Ships of the line were then separated in several classes, usually depending on the number of guns they boasted. Ships of the *first rate* numbered 100 guns each and were understandably, the finest of all. Nelson commanded over only 3 such ships in his fleet. *Second rate* ships were bearing 98 guns each, and there were 4 out them in the British fleet. The rest of Nelson's fleet was made up of a single 80-gun ship, 16 74-gun ships, and 3 64-gun ships.

In comparison, the combined fleet of the French and the Spanish outnumbered the British by quite a few ships. Their force numbered 33 vessels under the command of Pierre-Charles Villeneuve - six more than Nelson had. While this might sound like nothing much, in naval warfare, it counts as a lot. Four *first rates* were in the Spanish fleet, with two of them carrying 112 guns each, one carrying 100 guns, and one bearing an amazing 130 cannons - 30 more than the finest ship in Nelson's fleet, the HMS *Victory*. The rest of the Franco-Spanish fleet was made up from formidable vessels of which most carried 80 cannons. When we compare the setups of these two fleets, we can see that the fleet that Villeneuve commanded was superior in every way to that of Horatio Nelson. Nevertheless, he lacked the boldness, the tacticianship, and the skill that Nelson had.

However, one key thing stood as a clear line of separation between these two opposed fleets - crew skill. The British sailors and seamen were largely experienced veterans, used to the harsh conditions on board a warship. And harsh they were - life on a sailing boat of the era was notoriously inhumane. But the sailors in the French fleet were inexperienced, often freshly recruited, and requiring training on the go. This lack of experience for many of them largely stemmed from the fact that the ships they served on were blockaded for so long.

Cannons on their ship also played a critical role in this battle. Almost all of the cannons that the Franco-Spanish fleet boasted were fired by use of a *slow burning* fuse. Combine this fact with the crew's lack of experience, and you have an undesirable rate of fire of roughly 3 to 5 minutes for each shot.

The British on the other hand boasted cannons that relied on flintlock firing mechanisms. And with the experience of the cannon crews that manned them, they could achieve a rate of fire of just 90 seconds per shot.

Napoleon's orders were exact and clear, and even so, Villeneuve faltered. His task was to sail the combined fleet away from Cadiz and to Naples. However, Villeneuve once again grew indecisive, and changed the orders for his fleet several times in a span of a couple of days. In the end, he gave in to the pressures and gave the final order for his fleet to depart Cadiz on October 18th, 1805. But by then, it was perhaps too late. The weather was far from favorable, with only light winds and calm seas: this resulted in a very slow progress of the fleet. For the British however, this was a clear advantage, as they could easily observe the movements of their enemy.

As his fleet was reaching the open water, Villeneuve opted for a 3-line formation, stretching his column. However, just 2 days after departing Cadiz, he could spot to his rear the British fleet in pursuit. Villeneuve knew by this point that battle was imminent, and gave the order for a single line formation. By the next morning, the British were in full view to their rear, making swift pursuit with the wind filling their sails.

October 21st was the dawn of battle. On this day, the British fleet was situated roughly 34 kilometers to the northwest of the Cape Trafalgar on the Spanish coast. Between these two lay the combined Franco-Spanish fleet. Lord Admiral Horatio Nelson gave the order for full battle preparations around 6 AM on that day, and was in full view of the French just 2 hours later. It was at that point that Villeneuve decided to turn his entire fleet back and return to Cadiz - arguably a great mistake. His orders were not carried out effectively, and resulted in slow and uncoordinated turning. This resulted in a mixed formation and stretched line of ships that dragged on for around 8 kilometers. Nelson simply pressed on his advance and kept up the pursuit. He ordered a formation of two parallel lines, which were positioned as to cut directly into the center of the stretched fleet of his opponent. The only thing he could not recognize in the disorganized French fleet was their flagship. Here is where we can recognize the daring and calculated risks of a skilled naval commander: Nelson new that he was outgunned and outnumbered, but still exploited the situation and proceed onwards.

The battle was beginning around 11:45 that morning, and around that time Horatio Nelson issued his famous order that would become legendary. From the mizzen mast of his flagship HMS *Victory*, he ordered a message of naval coded signal flags that simply stated: *"England expects that every man will do his duty".*

And they sure did their duty. The parallel columns of the British fleet cut directly into the enemy ships, beginning the battle with catastrophic exchange of cannon volleys. What ensued was a chaotic naval battle, in which ships maneuver in search for the best possible angles of attack. HMS *Royal Sovereign*, the British 100 gun ship delivered an obliterating salvo from its cannons onto the Spanish *Santa Ana,* subsequently capturing it. Some ships, on the other hand, were less lucky. British HMS *Belleisle* faced four vessels at once, and was obliterated. This close quarter, violent battle was a classic example of the naval battle of the Napoleonic era: a chaotic battlefield where devastating cannon fire obliterated both ship and man, enveloping the scene in thick, fog-like gunpowder smoke. As formations grew tighter, the ships locked together and were boarded, pitting man against man in close quarter combat.

But throughout the struggle, the British fleet managed to retain an upper hand, continuously pressing their attack and exploiting the initial upper hand. As the rear of Nelson's formation entered the fray in succession, the Franco-Spanish fleet was put under constant pressure. In the end, the French and Spanish fleet - those that were not sunk - began surrendering. The British won the day.

Alas, it was a costly victory - Lord Admiral Horatio Nelson, one of the greatest commanders and heroes of the British, gave his life to a musket ball fired from an enemy ship. But his victory was enough to solidify British naval dominance: Napoleon's unfamiliarity with naval strategies and the incompetence of his commanders meant that he would never again gain the chance of crossing the channel.

The First Victories

SEVERAL KEY EVENTS marked the so-called War of the Third Coalition that lasted from 1803 to 1806. While the Battle of Trafalgar was certainly a crucial one, there were other events unfolding on the land that dictated the tempo of the Napoleonic Wars. And where Napoleon was not successful on the waters, he made up for it on the ground.

In 1804, Napoleon once more shocked the European world. He seized Louis Antoine de Bourbon, duc d'Enghien, a prominent French nobleman and the member of the wealthy House of Bourbon. The man was accused by Napoleon of aiding Britain and plotting against him, and subsequently charged and executed. This event caused widespread shock amongst the royal houses of Europe, and spurred Austria and Russia to act against Napoleon, essentially drawing them into war. The Russian Emperor, Tsar Alexander I entered the Third Coalition thus, wanting to put a stop to Napoleon's power.

The actual reasons of Duc d'Enghien's execution could have been even deeper, and a personal conflict between the two could have existed. Nevertheless, the action was - for many - a stain on Napoleon's honor.

Just as the sails on Trafalgar swelled and the cannons of the ships roared, a crucial engagement was also unfolding on land. In the so-called Ulm Campaign, Napoleon Bonaparte showed his exceptional skills as a military commander, pitting him against the Austrian Empire.

The latter began its military reforms as early as 1801, placing Field Marshal Karl Mack as the leading commander of the army. He too instigated reforms of the infantry, and this subsequently led to a good part of the officer core to lack sufficient training. Nevertheless, at the time of the Third Coalition, Austrians boasted some of the best cavalry forces in Europe. However, Napoleon was all about decisiveness. His tactics were swift, confident, straightforward, and often bold. His *Grande Armée* (The Great Army) numbered roughly 210,000 men at the time of the Ulm Campaign, split into seven army *corps.* He also secured a substantial cavalry reserve, with mixed dragoon and cuirassier divisions. One important advantage that the French army possessed was a well trained officer corps. Most if not all were veterans - serving in the preceding French Revolutionary Wars. On top of that, the French army was well equipped and well trained.

As the movements on the ground progressed, the Austrian commander Mack devised his own strategy. Considering the mountainous Black Forest area in Southern Germany the most viable path for Napoleon to exploit, he concentrated his defense of the Austrian borders there. He knew that he had the worst odds when facing Napoleon - his army numbered only 23,000 men. Thus he opted for defence, and for that chose the strategic town of Ulm. There, he hoped to stave off the French advance - if it came - and hold out long enough for the Russian reinforcements to arrive. The latter were on the march under General Kutuzov. But there was a great flaw in the Austrian thinking. As Napoleon's greatest focus in the preceding conflicts - in 1796 and 1800 - was on Italy, the Austrian command placed the bulk of their troops there, thinking that the French would strike there for the third time as well. However, Napoleon was not so unskilled a commander as they thought he was.

His intentions were thus: the seven corps of his Great Army - 210,000 troops - were to march to the East and hopefully envelop the Austrian forces under General Mack. To screen (hide) his movements, he relied on Marshal Murat, whose cavalry would confuse the Austrians, giving them the impression that Napoleon was in fact advancing in an opposite way. And all the while, he deftly secured all his weak points: Boulougne in coastal France was secured against a possible British invasion; Austrian troops in Italy were engaged and kept there; as were the forces in Naples. Furthermore, good communication lines and good reconnaissance made the execution of this plan even smoother.

Here, it is important to note that these are movements on a great scale. While reading these lines you might get an idea of a small-scale maneuver, in reality it was not so: these actions involved thousands upon thousands of men, and involved strategic deployments and movements that were numbered in tens of kilometers and involved many cities as key locations of an operation. Such was the "grand strategy" of the Napoleonic Era. After all, maneuvering with a force of 210,000 troops does require a bit of room.

The ensuing action was a textbook example of effective maneuvers and envelopment. Napoleon relied on a rapid, fast-paced march that he kept up often exceeding the capabilities of the infantry. Nevertheless, it allowed him to successfully conduct a large sweeping maneuver, wheeling behind the Austrian army of General Mack and capturing it by October 20th, 1805. In the entire Ulm Campaign, that lasted only 25 days, the French captured roughly 60,000 Austrian soldiers. The comparison of casualties is also quite differing: the French suffered 2,000 dead and wounded, and the Austrians close to 60,000. Napoleon could also rely on his highly competent generals, namely Marshal Murat and Marshal Ney, and also Marshal Davout. Their incentive, the swift movements, and reliability made the Ulm Campaign a sure success.

However, even though an entire Austrian army under Mack was captured, there still remained the threat of the arriving Russian army under Kutuzov. This large force was still close to Vienna in Austria, attempting to link up with the remnants of the Austrian army, and receive further reinforcements. It is at this crucial moment that Napoleon's decisiveness and perseverance paid off: he continued his advances, captured Vienna, and marched to face the Russians.

Battle of Austerlitz

THE WHOLE OF THE NAPOLEONIC Wars was filled with glorious battles, with skirmishes and clashes, with grand strategy and heroic exploits of soldiers and generals. However, one battle stood out as the absolute centerpiece of the entire era of Napoleonic Wars, a tactical masterpiece on a scale that was never before seen. Austerlitz is that battle, widely hailed as the crown jewel of Napoleon's entire life. It was etched onto the pages of history as a classic example of daring military strategy, of shrewd maneuvers and war of movement. Romanticized and storied in generations that followed, it was certainly a day of heroics. However, it was not so grandiose for the soldier on the field. Especially for the Austrian and Russian soldiers.

Following his triumph in the Ulm Campaign, and a swift capture of Mack's Austrian army, Napoleon kept up his pace, seizing Vienna in November 1805. Again he relied on feverish, highly rapid forced marches, aiming to attack the Russian army. The latter failed to relieve the Austrian forces under Mack, and now relocated to the northeast, awaiting reinforcements. At the head of the Russo-Austrian army was General Kutuzov, a man of great military prowess and the commander-in-chief appointed by the Russian Tsar Alexander. The Russian army boasted a highly skilled artillery force, priding itself on the extensive training its artillery crews had, and their veterancy. The common Russian infantryman was also hailed as a hardy and resilient soldier. However, the same could not be said for the Russian officer corps: the senior officers were almost exclusively recruited from within aristocratic circles. Princely families often saw prestige in military service, and officer commissions were often granted to the highest bidder or the higher noble. Competence played almost no role in the recruitment, and this resulted in a subpar officer corps.

As Napoleon continued his march toward the Russians, he realized the shortcomings of his position. First and foremost, were his communication lines. Stretched dangerously thin, they were in danger of cutting off, and required strengthened guard. With other difficulties in view, he knew that he *had* to draw the Russians into a battle if he was to capitalize the success he achieved at Ulm. However, Kutuzov was a shrewd commander. He too knew that Napoleon wanted a battle, and did not repeat the mistakes of General Mack. He retreated further to the east. And at this point is where the battle of the great military minds begins, with each general attempting to outsmart and "out-strategize" the other. Napoleon was always thinking ahead. He opted to lure the enemy to battle, laying a sort of psychological trap. For days preceding the battle, he did everything to present the French army as weakened, in disarray, and wishing peace. But all the while, he ordered roughly 53,000 men to occupy enemy attention and seize the Austerlitz heights and the Olmutz road. This was another lure - the Russo-Austrian army numbered roughly 89,000 men, and would find it tempting to attack the lesser French force.

But Napoleon craftily placed three armies - commanded by Davout, Mortier, and Bernadotte - at close distance, giving them the ability to quickly reinforce those 53,000 by a quick forced march. Furthermore, Napoleon emphasized his feint at wishing to avoid a battle by sending a respected commander - General Savary - to the headquarters of the enemy, expressing the desire to avoid a battle. This was supposed to look like a weakness. The Austrian Emperor Francis I soon after offered an armistice to Napoleon, which the latter (acting) enthusiastically accepted. Then he immediately ordered his troops to abandon the tactically advantageous heights at Austerlitz and Pratzen heights. He also ordered that this retreat be acted as chaotic and hasty.

Napoleon wanted the enemy to seize these grounds as a part of his plan. What's more, he took his ruse to a whole new level, when he expressed a desire to meet with the Russian Emperor Alexander. Instead, he received the Tsar's aide, Prince Dolgorukov. During that meeting Napoleon expressed a sense of indecisiveness, hesitation, and anxiety, in order to portray his situation as dire. It worked. After the meeting the Russians and the Austrians were certain of the French weakness, and most of the generals voted for an immediate attack on the French. The only one against it was the most experienced one - Kutuzov. He was, however, in minority, and his plans were rejected, causing the Russians and Austrians to fall headfirst into Napoleon's daring trap.

The Battle of Austerlitz took place roughly ten kilometers (six miles) to the south east of the second-largest city in modern day Czech Republic - Brno. In 1805, however, it was a part of Austria. As the name suggests, it was situated in the vicinity of the town of Austerlitz (today known as *Slavkov u Brna*), with the main happening at the gently sloping hill known as Pratzen Heights. On the morn of battle, Napoleon was outnumbered: at his disposal was around 72,000 men, with another 7,000 under Marshal Davout further to the south. The Russians and Austrians on the other hand, boasted 85,000 men and roughly double the artillery - 318 guns against Napoleon's 157.

Napoleon then performed one of his biggest gambles - in order to encourage the enemy to attack, he purposefully made his right flank weaker. It is clear here that he was a daring risk taker: he himself was uncertain of victory, as were his Marshals. On 28th of November, they gathered at the headquarters, where they encouraged a retreat. Napoleon rejected this, and stuck to his bold plan: seeing his weakened flank, the enemy would swiftly concentrate a large force in hopes of enveloping him and cut the lines of communication. However - this action would leave the enemy center and the left flank vulnerable. During all this, Napoleon would hide the bulk of his force opposite the Pratzen heights which he previously abandoned. The plan dictated that this main force was to exploit the weakened center of the enemy, and encircle their army from the rear. A lot of what this plan was about had to do with the layout of the land - using it in an effective manner, a military commander could greatly tip the scales in his own favor.

The battle proper began around 8 AM on December 2nd, 1805. That morning was in particular cold and misty. From the first volleys exchanged, the battle was proving to be fierce in every regard. Several small villages and towns dotted the area of Austerlitz, and many of them saw heavy fighting. As Napoleon predicted, the enemy forces began decisively attacking the French right flank with mounting pressures, but slowly at first. During the battle, Kutuzov once again proved his maturity and skill as a commander, when he too - just like Napoleon - understood the clear importance of the Pratzen Heights, and placed his IVth Corps directly onto it, in wait. However, the somewhat impatient and young Russian Emperor, Alexander, failed to recognize the hill's worth, and thus ordered Kutuzov to abandon the heights. This decision sealed the fate of the Russian and Austrian armies.

By 8:45 in the morning, Napoleon could finally spot that which he planned all along - a weakened enemy center. He promptly ordered Marshal Soult to hastily march his men to the Pratzen Heights, famously stating: "*One sharp blow, and the war is over*".

It was the division under the command of General Saint-Hilaire that made the push to the heights, surprising the Russian remnants on top of it in a vicious attack. It was a ferocious and bitter struggle to take this position, but eventually Saint-Hilaire's men managed to drive the enemy away from the Pratzen Heights after final hand to hand combat. Meanwhile, the battle elsewhere was steadily going in France's favor. The Russians quickly grasped the difficulty of their position - this was certain once they deployed their heavy cavalry, the Russian Imperial Guard, which was commanded by the Emperor's own brother, Grand Duke Constantine. These were highly competent soldiers, and their vicious attack resulted in the capture of a single French standard - the only one lost that day.

Napoleon swiftly reacted to this significant threat, ordering his own heavy Guard Cavalry to ride to attack. They faced the Russian cavalry, and in the ensuing clash completely obliterated them. This goes to show just how more experienced the French cavalrymen were. The French artillery also played a crucial role in this battle. The horse-drawn cannons were a mobile and efficient weapon, and inflicted heavy casualties on the Russian in several stages of the battle. The Pratzen heights were especially bloody in this regard, and even the Russian General Kutuzov was wounded there.

Throughout most of the battle, the Russians had numerical advantage. Several Russian maneuvers at the start were executed too slowly and failed to reach adequate position. However, when they fixed themselves later on, their slowness proved to be a boon - since they thus acted as reinforcement to the depleting Russian numbers on the north of the battlefield. Nevertheless, with crucial deployments from the French Marshal Murat, and the exceptional prowess of the French soldiers, the forces of Napoleon held the field. To the south of the battlefield, where Napoleon later shifted his attention, the fortress of Sokolnitz played a key role - it exchanged hands several times during the battle. However, the relocated division of Saint Hillaire, alongside the 3rd Corps of Marshal Davout, attacked Sokolnitz in a decisive two pronged formation, forcing the enemy to flee in panic after bitter fighting. Most (in)famously, the commander of the Russian left flank, the seasoned commander Von Buxhowden, was thoroughly drunk, and also joined in the retreat with his forces. Step by step, the French prevailed, and soon enough, the Russo-Austrian forces began an all-out panicked retreat.

The defeat at the Battle of Austerlitz was an absolute disaster for all Allied powers. Since the War of the Third Coalition was essentially British-led, it caused a great wave of doubt in their ability. Napoleon achieved what he desired - he was hailed as a hero by his men, and his victory was recognized by all as an absolute tactical wonder. The ferocity of the fighting, and the magnitude of his victory essentially hastened the end of the War of the Third Coalition. Almost immediately after his victory, Napoleon signed the *Treaty of Pressburg* with the Austrians. The result of the treaty was the withdrawal of Austria from the Third Coalition, and its essential surrender - it was eliminated from the entire war. It also lost a good deal of territories, which passed on to the French. But arguably the most important change that came out of the treaty of Pressburg and as a consequence of Austerlitz is the dissolution of the Holy Roman Empire after centuries of existence. It was replaced by the Confederation of the Rhine, created by Napoleon. Such was the power and the deafening echo of Napoleon's incredible victory at Austerlitz. Through sheer competence, through cunning and skill as a military commander, he managed to deal a crippling blow to Austria, and also send the Russian's fleeing with tails tucked between their legs. Nevertheless, although the War of the Third Coalition was essentially over after that, the Napoleonic Wars as a whole were not. The Kingdom of Prussia, whose intentions in the European conflict were uncertain up to that point, now began to seriously worry about Napoleon and his rapid expansion through Central Europe. Their *"entry into the fray"* led to the formation of a new coalition of allied powers, and thus brought to the War of the Fourth Coalition in 1806.

Chapter IV
Strong as Iron
The War of the Fourth Coalition

JUST A FEW MONTHS FOLLOWING the devastating collapse of the Third Coalition at the hands of Napoleon, the so-called *Allied* powers - i.e those who were Napoleon's enemies - formed the Fourth Coalition. This time, it was composed of Britain, Saxony, Sweden, Russia, and Prussia. It is crucial to remember here that Napoleon was not keen on continuing the conflict, at least not immediately. He was mostly aiming for a general peace in Europe - arguably, on his own terms - especially due to the fact that he still faced two major opponents, Britain and Russia. But even so, he sought to place Prussia "to the side", and thus removing it as a possible enemy. To keep it away from the influence of both Russia and Britain, and to contain its political and military rise amongst the German states, he offered a hasty and provisional alliance.

However, the enemies of Napoleon were unwilling to back down and submit to peace. One crucial factor stood in between them, and was used by the allies as a fresh reason for continued war against Napoleon. And that factor was the German electorate of Hanover. Since it was in personal union with the British monarchy, it was a key source of dispute, due to the fact that it was occupied by France. Continued contention over this point would gradually turn into the reason for war for Britain and Prussia against Napoleon. Sweden was also dragged onto their side, whose forces remained in Hanover from the previous conflict. With mounting tensions, it seemed impossible that war could be prevented, so shortly after the devastation of the War of the Third Coalition.

The War of the Fourth Coalition began roughly in October 1806, and lasted until July 1807 - less than a year. The official start of the war was preceded by some minor clashes which had no lasting impact on either Napoleon or his enemies. In fact, during this entire period, Britain and France were not involved in direct military clashes. Their conflicts in this period were mostly economic.

For Russia on the other hand, 1806 was spent on healing from the crushing defeat it received at Austerlitz. Nevertheless, it was still a huge opponent for Napoleon, and one of his biggest obstacles. The Russian Empire was notorious for the amount of manpower it could muster, as well for the hardiness of its troops.

Another crucial contributor to the formation of the Fourth Coalition was without a doubt the so-called Confederation of the Rhine, which was formed in July of 1806 by Napoleon, following his triumph in the War of the Third Coalition. This was - as the name suggests - a confederation of several German states of the Rhineland and extended west Germany, which acted as a crucial "buffer zone" between Napoleon's France and the East. This was of course a satellite, puppet state of the French Empire, and led directly to the dissolution of the already venerable Holy Roman Empire. Here we can observe a shrewd and mature move by Napoleon - one of many he made. Since the Holy Roman Empire was largely composed of various small states, he consolidated them into larger duchies and electorates, in order to make the governing of this confederation efficient and easier. What is more, his two major allies of these German states were Bavaria and Württemberg - both of them he raised to the status of Kingdoms. But have no doubt - the purpose of the Confederation of the Rhine was almost entirely a military one. Napoleon provides to them "protection", and the states provide a stellar amount of auxiliary troops and valuable resources. The Confederation of the Rhine acted largely as a buffer against Prussia - which by now was becoming increasingly disapproving of French actions and their spread towards the east. The tensions between the two finally escalated to a state of war in 1806, when the French arrested and summarily executed a prominent German nationalist - Johann Philipp Palm. The man was instrumental in publishing a strongly anti-Napoleon pamphlet and attacking him. Following this, Prussia and France went to war.

The Prussian decision was resting on the shoulders of only its King - Friedrich Wilhelm III. He made this decision independently of any other major power, but was nevertheless influenced by outside elements, namely his own wife - the idealized and influential Queen Louise - and also the war party in Berlin. Prussia was also supposed to have entered the war even earlier, during the War of the Third Coalition, joining forces with Austria and Russia. There were even considerable negotiations between the Emperor of Russia and the Prussian King in years before 1805, where a secret coalition against Napoleon was made by these two rulers. However, as the war broke out, Prussia was indecisive and wavered on two sides, eventually declaring neutrality in a very hasty way. If they chose not to do so, the disaster at Austerlitz could have been prevented with the help of the Prussian army. However this did not occur, and Napoleon triumphed instead.

But now, with the Fourth Coalition made, Prussia became a valuable ally to the Russians - and a grave enemy of Napoleon. One thing stood between them though, and that was the sheer distance: Russians were still a long ways away, hastily remobilizing their troops and recovering from their previous defeat.

The only ally the Prussians had close by was also their only German ally - the state of Saxony. For Napoleon, it seemed so foolish and ill-conceived that Prussia would face his *Grande Armee* with just Saxony at its side, and Russia so far away. All the while, the animosity between the French and Prussian soldiers grew steadily, with plenty of blames going back and forth and nationalistic pride swelling, setting the stage for the coming conflict and rousing the men to fight. Strategically however, Napoleon placed the great bulk of his forces all along the border with South Saxony, when he realised that conflict is all but inevitable. This was the very core of his Great Army. This mass of troops he then marched through the massive Franconian woods of south Thuringia, in the so-called "battalion square" of three great parallel columns. With these maneuvers, he hoped for a pre-emptive strike that would catch the Prussian forces by surprise, giving him an initial upper hand. Tactically, this was a sound plan - each of these columns was in supporting distance of one another, allowing for full focus of forces against any possible attack. Napoleon opted for this tactic due to having almost no information of the Prussian army's positions or size at the time.

Once more, Napoleon's brilliance as a strategist and commander comes to the forefront - he had no sure knowledge of the enemy's positions, but still managed to correctly guess that their main bulk would be concentrated somewhere in the vicinity of Erfurt. Following this belief, he created a sound plan, where he would make a main thrust down the valley of the river Saale, and thus making his trusted enveloping approach, with which the left flank of the Prussian army (if indeed they were where he believed) would be enveloped, and their communications and line of retreat cut off. This led to the famous Jena-Auerstedt Campaign of October 1806.

The Battles of Jena-Auerstedt

UP TO THAT POINT, NAPOLEON'S victory at the Battle of Austerlitz was hailed as one of his crowning achievements. However, he would soon prove that it was only the first such in a series of many more: the triumphs in the twin battles of Jena and Auerstedt would come to be some of his finest.

The initial clashes of this campaign began on October 9th, 1806, starting with the smaller Battle of Schleiz. It was the first fight of the War of the Fourth Coalition, in which the French forces engaged a Prussian division under the command of General Bogislav von Tauentzien. The engagement proved to be the partial guess of Napoleon's initial assessment - the Grande Armee struck the Prussian Army's left wing as they advanced through the Franconian woods. The initial strikes pitched the forces of French Marshal Drouet and of Prussian General von Tauentzien against one another, but the latter soon found out that he was heavily outnumbered, commencing a tactical retreat. The Prussians suffered heavy losses here, and also their first defeat. On the very next day, the Battle of Saalfeld brought the French yet another victory. In it, the French Marshal Jean Lannes faced a force of Prussians commanded by the popular Prince Louis Ferdinand of Prussia, who lost his life in this battle, and in a glorious manner.

On 14th of October, the main elements of Napoleon's *Grande Armee* were getting in contact with the 38,000 strong Prussian force near Jena, under the command of Frederick Louis, Prince of Hohenlohe. The battle began in the early morning hours, marked by the initial movements by the French army in order to attack the flanks of the Prussians. These maneuvers allowed for the central portion of Napoleon's forces to get into suitable position in time. In the opening skirmishes of the Battle of Jena, little was achieved on either side. However, one risky action by Napoleon's trusted Marshal Michel Ney could have proven to be a costly failure for the French. It happened when Ney finally brought up the center into position. But once he did so, instead of waiting for further orders from Napoleon, he proceeded to attack the central Prussian line of his own accord. While his forces quickly made progress in the attack, Ney quickly realized his blunder, with having his forces over-extended: a classic military error. The Prussians realized this mistake and quickly enveloped Ney's forces. Not unlike the Romans of ancient history, Ney placed his forces into a square position, hoping to protect all of his sides. But, Napoleon acted with composure and sound strategy: To relieve the enveloped Marshal Ney, he shifted his forces under Marshal Lannes to Ney. But since this action weakened the French center, Napoleon deployed his trusty and vicious Imperial Guard to hold the center until the situation with Ney was resolved. With an almost textbook *"relief"* operation, Napoleon once more proven his adjustability in the heat of battle, and the exceptional ability to adapt to the immediate situation. Ney and his forces were successfully rescued and allowed to retreat from the field.

However, this entire situation was never fully exploited by the Prussian command: they were slow to react to the developments on the field, and when they did, they were equally slow to react accordingly. This was ultimately what brought to their failure. The slowness of some Prussian positions led to vicious fighting, exposing men to artillery without an effective way to fight back.

By 1 PM, Napoleon recognized his opponent's lack of decisiveness, and thus took the initiative of the battle, making his winning move. He ordered both of his flanks, as well as his center to press the attacks hard on the Prussians, hoping to break them and encircle their core. It was a successful move, with the Prussian flanks breaking under pressure and their troops mass-fleeing the battlefield in an all-out retreat. Hohenlohe's force suffered heavy casualties, even as they fled. It was another fantastic victory for the French.

At the very same time a battle was brewing near Auerstedt not too far from Jena. As the Battle of Jena was underway Marshal Davout and General Bernadotte were requested to move their forces to the south in order to aid Napoleon. Davout took the route via Eckartsberga, while Bernadotte took the route via Dornburg. The former's path however, was blocked by the main Prussian army, headed with the Prussian King himself. At his side were also the famed Duke of Brunswick, and the Prussian Field Marshals von Kalckreuth and von Muellendorf. The stage was set for another decisive engagement - so close to Napoleon at Jena. Luckily, Davout was a skilled commander, and the forces under his command were equally seasoned and hardy. When Marshal Davout grasped the situation and recognized the size of the Prussian force, he ordered his General Gudin and his division to deploy near the village of Hassenhausen. Field Marshal von Shmettau was deployed against him, with his troops quickly setting to attack Hassenhausen. Gudin was then placed into a difficult position, especially after the arrival of Bluecher and his cavalry troops. This pushed him out of the village after a fierce clash. Around 8:30 AM, Prussian forces under the Duke of Brunswick arrived as well, and were positioned on the left (infantry) and the right flank (cavalry). However, by 9 AM the French deployed their cavalry to the left of Gudin's positions, and by half an hour later, the French artillery was also in position, on the right of Gudin. This made the setup of the Battle of Auerstedt. French forces - deployed in protective square formations - soon forced the Prussian cavalry to a retreat, advancing all the while. Soon after, things went awry for the Prussians. Seeing three of their cavalry regiments fleeing, the Prussian infantry also fell back. By 10 AM, the situation became dire, and the Duke of Brunswick desperately sought a solution. He ordered a full assault, but to no avail. He himself was struck by a musket ball and lost both of his eyes, and had to be carried from the battle. He died roughly a month later. His second-in-command was Karl von Schmettau, who was likewise mortally wounded. This lack of command caused a major breakdown amongst the Prussian command. On the other hand, by 11 AM the seasoned Marshal Davout could see that the Prussians were see-sawing on the brink of collapse, and promptly ordered a counter-attack. Just an hour later, the Prussian army was in shambles, with their center broken and in retreat, their cavalry decimated, and morale low. The Prussian King thus saw the situation and ordered a full retreat.

Although severely outnumbered, Davout's seasoned men and officers managed to win the day, cementing the victory at Jena-Auerstedt decisively. Napoleon had much to thank the III Corps, which Davout commanded over. This unit was one of the finest in his employ, and came to prominence between the years of 1805 and 1809, repeatedly scoring numerous victories and gaining notoriety for hardiness and military prowess. Napoleon affectionately called it "*My Tenth Legion*", in reference to the Roman *Legio X Gemina*, under the command of Julius Caesar. However, both sides engaged at Auerstedt suffered heavy casualties.

Davout's masterful conduct at Auerstedt and the incredible victory he achieved there came as a surprise for Napoleon. After all, it was just the single III Corps that managed to defeat the numerically far superior Prussian main force, owing to general disbelief. When first hearing the reports of this victory, Napoleon famously responded: "*Your Marshal [Davout] must be seeing double!*" This referred to the poor eyesight Davout was known to have had. But when it became certain that Davout won a great victory, Napoleon showered him with praise and honours, making him the Duke of Auerstedt. All of it deservedly.

The victory at Jena-Auerstedt, was however not the end. Marshal Joakim Murat continued to pursue the Prussians with his cavalry units, and the latter was in no way able to mount a significant resistance, especially with their two major commanders being mortally wounded. This pursuit led to the Capitulation of Erfurt on October 16th, two days after the battle, where a large number of Prussian troops surrendered to Murat. Even so, the Prussians were not out of the game yet. However, with their capital, Berlin, falling soon, things were not looking well. Napoleon granted the celebrated Marshal Davout the privilege of entering Berlin first, which he did with his III Corps on October 25th. Three days later, Joakim Murat intercepted a Prussian force under the command of Hohenlohe at the Battle of Prenzlau, whereupon the latter surrendered to the French. Napoleon kept up his pursuit of the Prussian remnants, and the days following Jena-Auerstedt were marked with numerous Prussian defeats and capitulations, notably at Anklam on November 1st, and Wismar on November 5th. However, one final Prussian force remained in the field, and that was the 21,000 strong army under the command of General Field Marshal Gebhard von Blücher. He was tirelessly pursued across the country by Marshals Murat, Bernadotte, and Soult.

Seeking a solution to his situation with mounting desperation, von Blücher entered the neutral city of Lübeck, which was a key town of the Hanseatic League. He promptly fortified it and hoped to rely on its ships to make his escape. However, Bernadotte put a wrench in the cogs of his plan, when the French surrounded the city and destroyed the Prussian force in the *Battle of Lübeck* on November 6 and 7th.

The battle was a risky operation by the French, but successful nonetheless. Von Blücher surrendered to the French Marshal after seeing the hopelessness of his situation. The Prussians suffered around 3000 casualties, and many more went into captivity. This effectively ended Prussian resistance, and put them out of the war.

Napoleon's mastery in the field, and his cool-headed command in the heat of battle were the defining factors of his victories. It is important to note that at the time of the battle of Jena, Napoleon commanded over a force of roughly 116,000 - but he deployed only around 40,000. One historian carefully put this into perspective:

"Napoleon at Jena had known nothing about the main action that took place on that day; had forgotten all about two of his corps; did not issue orders to a third, and possibly a fourth; was taken by surprise by the action of a fifth; and, to cap it all, had one of his principal subordinates display the kind of disobedience that would have brought a lesser mortal before a firing squad. Despite all these faults in command, Napoleon won what was probably the great single triumph in his career."

The crucial detail of this whole conflict that we need to take into account is the simple fact that it took Napoleon just 19 days to essentially knock Prussia out of the war after invading their territory. This serves as yet another testament to the rapidity of his warfare, and the expertise of his seasoned troops. And, of course, it goes much to put shame on the Prussians, who lost the conflict in such a record time - and so definitely. What little remained from its armies fled to East Prussia where they would link up with the approaching Russian army. Saxony on the other hand, chose the easy way out - allying itself with Napoleon and getting elevated to the status of a Kingdom and entering the buffer zone of the Confederation of the Rhine.

Another crucial outcome of this campaign was the issuing of the Berlin Decree by Napoleon. This was his way to put the Continental System into action - a specially designed foreign policy that was to serve as an answer to the British naval blockade. It was a key part of the economic struggle between the two powers, and served as a large scaled embargo against British goods and trade. The British exports to mainland Europe dropped by half between 1802 and 1806. The decree further affected it by forbidding the import of British goods into any European countries which were allied or dependent on France. The decree went so far as to cut mail connections with Britain. Nevertheless, the Continental Blockade did little to harm the British economy, as trade continued through extensive smuggling networks.

Furthermore, the economies of France and many of its allied nations were affected by the system, due to the fact that they lost a major trading partner. Later on in the Napoleonic Wars, the Continental System would actually work as a weakening factor of Napoleon's coalition - his major allies became increasingly agitated at the losses it brought, and gained an incentive to ignore it altogether.

However, Prussians suffering a defeat did not mean that the War of the Fourth Coalition was over. Russians still remained to be faced. At the end of 1806 and early weeks of 1807, Napoleon entered Poland and created the so-called Duchy of Warsaw, another client state of the French Empire. Following this, the Russians gained the incentive for an offensive into East Prussia. Napoleon likewise marched to face the enemy and turned to the north-east, in hopes of conquering Königsberg, the "new capital" of the Prussians, and also facing the Russian threat. In the winter days of late January 1807, the Russian army under the command of Levin von Bennigsen began its offensive and made quick progress to the west.

Napoleon reacted by a counter-offensive, with his aim being to cut off Russian lines of retreat to the east. However, in a turn of events, the daring Russian Cossack troops managed to capture a copy of Napoleon's orders, realizing his intentions. The Russian command promptly retreated to the north in order not to be cut off and enveloped, and Napoleon pursued. Several days later, the French forces came upon the Russians prepared for battle near the town of Preußisch Eylau (known commonly then as Eylau), some 37 kilometers from Königsberg. The ensuing clash became the Battle of Eylau.

Eylau lasted from 7th to 8th of February 1807, and was largely an inconclusive battle, which came as the first major test for the French army, and placed Napoleon's reputation for invincibility to the test. The battle was also one of the bloodiest in both the War of the Fourth Coalition and the Napoleonic Wars as a whole.

It was preceded by several days of complex maneuvering and minor clashes, as the Russian commander, Bennigsen, attempted to reposition the bulk of his army in order to surprise the French. The battle eventually escalated in and around the city of Eylau, with some of the most ferocious and brutal fighting to be seen up to that point. In the evening of the first day, the French managed to capture the small town, with both sides suffering catastrophic casualties. However, the fighting on the following day was in many ways even more fierce. Napoleon attempted a daring and risky frontal attack which failed with great losses suffered. Trying to fix this error, Napoleon launched a massive cavalry attack against the Russian lines. The so-called "Cavalry charge at Eylau" became one of the greatest cavalry attacks in military history. But it was also a bloody and barbaric fight in many regards. The charge gave the French right flank to position itself and enter the fray, bringing the Russian army close to collapse. However, the latter was saved by a newly arriving Prussian corps that threatened the French right flank in earnest. Nevertheless, with the late evening appearance of yet another French corps on the left flank, Russian General Bennigsen made the decision to retreat. The battle was neither won nor lost. All that Napoleon gained at Eylau was a snowy expanse - a scarred battlefield littered with blood and corpses. Marshal Ney famously stated that it was a "massacre, without any result gained", and was a strategically inconclusive battle. Both sides suffered well over 20,000 casualties.

It is crucial to note that the Battle of Eylau cannot be effectively summarized in the confines of this book. It is without a doubt one of the most complex engagements in the Napoleonic Wars, and was defined by masterful strategic maneuvers and complicated operation on the field.

Nevertheless, Napoleon managed to redeem himself with the coming of the spring. After the massacre that was the Battle of Eylau, the French forces spent the remainder of the winter recuperating.

However, as the weather turned to spring again, Napoleon ordered a general move on once again. He subsequently learned that the Russians have made their camp at the town of Heilsberg, and incorrectly assumed that it was merely the rearguard. In the smaller Battle of Heilsberg, Napoleon learned that it was not the rearguard that he found, but the entire Russian army, numbering well over 50,000 men - well entrenched. His repeated attacks failed to move the Russians and caused high casualties, but eventually led to the Russians abandoning the town. Napoleon naturally pursued, and once more came upon their camps at Friedland. Here, the Russian commander Bennigsen made a grave error, and misjudged the French forces he spotted, choosing to engage what he thought was simply their flank. By moving his entire force across the Alle river to engage this force, he made a grave error. The French managed to hold out against the Russians as Napoleon brought the remainder of his forces into the fray. With his recognizable decisiveness, Napoleon launched one massive focused attack and broke the Russian defenses, trapping them against the river. The Russians broke and began an all out panicked retreat, with many men drowning in the process.

Friedland was another decisive victory for Napoleon, and a strategic necessity after the inconclusive bloodshed at Eylau. His casualties here were close to 10,000 men, but the Russians fared far, far worse, suffering catastrophic casualties with close to 40,000 men lost - 40% of their soldiers on the battlefield.

What is more, after losing at Friedland the Russian Emperor was promptly convinced that peace was needed and fast. And that peace was the Treaty of Tilsit - much to Napoleon's benefit. This in essence brought the end of the War of the Fourth Coalition, and gave Napoleon not just another victory under his belt, but also a lot of territorial gains: Prussia lost almost half of its territories, and Russia joined the aforementioned Continental System. The gained Prussian lands were turned into another client state of the French Empire, the

Kingdom of Westphalia - securing the absolute French domination of Europe and bringing Napoleon's Empire to its greatest heights.

Chapter V
A Spark in Iberia
The Peninsular War, 1808-1814

JUST AS NAPOLEON'S triumphs against the Prussians and the Russians were reaching their crescendo, bringing the Fourth Coalition to its end, events on the Iberian Peninsula were unfolding dazzlingly fast, threatening to spill over into a whole new conflict. In truth, both Spain and Portugal were nations deeply divided, enveloped in turmoil and a clash of generations and mentalities that was anything but harmless. And this deep divide would turn into one of the biggest and longest conflicts within the Napoleonic Wars. This conflict would come to be known as the Peninsular War, and would last from May 1808 to April 1814.

After his successful campaigns in Prussia, and a treaty with the Russians secured, Napoleon turned his gaze towards Portugal. In truth, he was vexed with it: Portugal still actively engaged in trade with Britain, and was also its oldest ally in Europe. This alliance was made far back in 1386, and lasts to this day as one of the oldest formal alliances in the world. But for Napoleon, this friendship was anything but acceptable. Not only did Britain have a foothold in mainland Europe, but also heavily relied on Portugal's ports in Lisbon, as well as its Brazilian colonies. Napoleon further lost his temper when the Portuguese regent, Prince John of Braganza, declined to bring Portugal within the Continental System to block British trade and economy. All of this gave Napoleon plenty of pretexts and reasons to make Portugal his new enemy in Europe.

Spain too was becoming a thorn in the French side. At the beginning of the Napoleonic Wars, Spain was a loyal ally of Napoleon. However, after the crippling defeat at Trafalgar, with the majority of their fleet obliterated, the Spaniards began to doubt the importance of this alliance and failed to find valid reasons for its continued existence. Tensions grew further at the beginning of the War of the Fourth Coalition, when Spain's First Secretary of State, Godoy, issued a jarring proclamation against France. Napoleon's suspicions grew and he knew that Spain had become a wavering ally at best. He knew that he would need to deal with it as well.

By mid to late 1807, events began unfolding that no one would be able to stop. Napoleon made his move against Portugal in July of that year, ordering his Foreign Minister, Charles de Talleyrand, to order Portugal to declare war on Britain. Furthermore, it was to close its ports for all and any British vessels, to seize British goods, and detain all British subjects. Needless to say, Napoleon knew that the Portuguese would not accept these terms, and began concentrating his troops at Bayonne in Southwest France. When the Portuguese government denied to comply, Napoleon had all the reasons he needed for an invasion. His armies were commanded by General Junot, who was ordered to cross into the Spanish Empire and march from there to the Portuguese capital of Lisbon. Junot was instructed by his Emperor to make haste - British intervention in Portugal was a distinct possibility. Lisbon was thus occupied by the French on November 30th 1807.

Following the French invasion, the Portuguese royal family fled in absolute disarray. The Prince regent gathered his family, nobles of the royal court, his treasure and important papers, and hastily embarked on a small fleet and sailed to Brazil. His elopement was so hasty and fear-driven, that much of his goods were left behind on the docks. With the French occupation complete, it was a matter of subjecting the populace. While the authorities were accepting of the new rule, the common folk was not, and resentment rose throughout the populace.

The French introduced high taxes, and this was met with wide unrest. By early 1808, civilians were executed when trying to resist. And Napoleon knew that such widespread unrest can quickly turn into an armed and dangerous rebellion.

Things on the Iberian Peninsula were unfolding quickly in 1808. In Early February, the French divisions crossed over into Spain, and hastily occupied Catalonia and Navarre, with their strategically important forts at Barcelona and Pamplona. A lot of confusion arose from this - as the two were still allied, and the French troops came announcing their marches and waving their flags. Thus, when credible explanations were not given, the Secretary of State Godoy responded by pulling out all Spanish troops out of Portugal, leaving the French on their own. However, by 20th of February, Napoleon appointed his trusted Marshal Joachim Murat as the commander of all French troops in Spain. Those troops were known as the Army of Spain and numbered between 60,000 and 100,000 men. Things escalated further when the populace of Madrid rose in rebellion against the French occupation. Marshal Murat responded with the deployment of his heavy, elite Imperial Guard cavalry which put down the rebellion in a brutal manner, trampling the rioters. On the following day, hundreds of Madrid citizens were shot by French firing squads as reprisal. For days after, shootings and executions followed in other Spanish cities. With that began Spain's *guerilla,* a vicious fight against the French occupation and all those who supported it.

By late May, numerous big Spanish cities erupted in violent uprising: Zaragoza, Valencia, Murcia. The province of Asturias declared war on the French Empire by May 25th, with all other provinces of Spain quickly following its example. Seeing the proud Spanish reaction, Portugal felt inspired and by June of that year it too revolted fully. Napoleon had his war in Iberia.

The Peninsular War turned out to be a lengthy and complicated conflict, with numerous ups and downs and complicated political evolutions. Summarizing it is certainly a challenge, and to present it in detail could easily require a book of its own. It was marked with numerous battles, many of which presented a challenge for Napoleon. Some of the initial battles against the Spanish were two minor battles at *El Bruc* against Catalan irregular militia. These opening stages of the conflict were marked by stalemates and French failures. What is more, the French army suffered its first defeat in a land battle in the Napoleonic Wars - surrendering at the Battle of Bailen. Further failures included the unsuccessful storming of Girona, the failed attack on Zaragoza and Valencia, and also the mass casualties amongst raw French recruits.

French dominance was at last shaken after the defeat at Bailen, marking the totality of their failure on the Iberian Peninsula. Losing close to 24,000 troops in those initial months, Napoleon experienced the bitterness of failure in earnest this time, as his military might in Spain came to a grinding halt. By August the French Army retreated to safer positions behind the Ebro river - that historic border. Parallel to the developments in the Peninsular War, the War of the Fifth Coalition broke out in 1809, set into motion after the defeat at Bailen. Of this war we shall write in detail.

It is however, important to note that the Peninsular War was perhaps the first serious British involvement on land in the Napoleonic Wars. Standing on the side of their age-old ally Portugal, the British began a lengthy campaign in order to at last get a foothold on the mainland, secure their military power and attempt to liberate Spain and Portugal from Napoleon. Sir Arthur Wellesley, Lieutenant-General of the British Army, was the first to land in Portugal at the head of 15,000 seasoned soldiers. He would go on to achieve two initial victories, at Roliça on August 17th, and against Junot at Vimeiro.

In the meantime, Napoleon was on full alert. After Bailen and the loss of Portugal, his *Armée d'Espagne* (Army of Spain) numbered roughly 279,000 men, secure beyond the Ebro. Opposite to them were some 88,000 Spanish soldiers. However, those troops were mostly raw recruits, lacking considerable organization. Napoleon exploited this in late 1808, relying on his envelopment tactics to defeat the Spanish defenses at Tudela, Espinosa, Burgos, and Somosierra, and going on to re-conquer Madrid by December 1st. Most of early to mid 1809 was thus spent in constant warfare, with back and forth progress by both sides. The French initially scored a series of victories, but were however defeated at few turns, being forced to hastily retreat along the way. This war had a devastating effect on Spain (Portugal too) which has been thoroughly ransacked, and destabilized to its core. Its Church was in shambles, and the society in a state of turmoil. Even after the Peninsular War was over, Spain was divided, and its two clashing parties descended into the Carlist Wars. All together, these several years of conflict left an irreversible mark on Spain's history, remaining as one of the worst periods to befall it. In some respects, it was even worse than the debilitating Spanish Civil War of the 20th century.

By 1810, the Cortes of Cádiz emerged as a reconstituted national government, or better yet, a government-in-exile, and fortified itself in the port of Cádiz. The combined Anglo-Portuguese force eventually secured the whole of Portugal, and it became their "safe harbor", and a springboard for operations against the French. Sir Arthur Wellesley, later to be the Duke of Wellington, was instrumental in the protection of Portugal, and also for reforming the demoralized Portuguese army. This was the key factor that prolonged the Peninsular War up to 1814, and the years of conflict were marked by relative stalemate and the inability of the French to make significant progress in Spain.

The Anglo-Portuguese army exploited Napoleon's 1812 invasion of Russia by pushing deep into Spain under the command of Wellesley, landing a big defeat on the French at Salamanca and one more retaking Madrid, the capital. This was then emphasized in 1813 with Duke of Wellington's impressive victory over the army of Joseph Bonaparte at the Battle of Vitoria on June 21st 1813, which was marked with high casualties, but cemented Wellington's name as one of the big threats to the French. By that time, the French Empire was no longer as strong as in 1808, and eventually Marshal Soult, without sufficient support, withdrew out of Spain across the Pyrenees Mountains in the Winter of 1813 on 1814.

It can be safely said that the Peninsular War was that tiny drop of water that worked away the stone that was Napoleon. It was the conflict that the French Empire did not need, and in a way worked towards its downfall. Besides the failed invasion of Russia, the Peninsular War was the next catastrophic episode for Napoleon, one that would cost him dearly in the end. Spain proved to be unlike anything in Northeastern Europe, and the French Great Army was to experience it firsthand. By the end, it was severely exhausted and overstrained. One crucial catalyst for its failure was the Spanish *guerilla* warfare. Where the French excelled at grand battles and strategic mastery, the Spanish excelled at intermittent warfare, in raids, ambushes, and harassment. And that was something that the French Marshals were not accustomed to. Such warfare greatly demoralized the French troops, but even more importantly, steadily drained the resources of the French army. By the end, Napoleon realized that instigating a war with Portugal proved to be a disastrous error, and that Spain was to be crucial in his defeat.

However, the Peninsular War was perhaps a "ugly necessity" for Spain to resolve its internal conflicts and separation. Just like in the years preceding the Second World War when the Spanish Civil War crippled this nation, the Peninsular War was equally a catalyst to bring forward reforms. In 1812 the Spanish Constitution was brought, and would later become the crucial part of European liberalism. Nevertheless, the massive strain on both Portugal and Spain, and the devastation caused by the war would lead to several years of economic stagnation, social unrest, and massive political instability. Civil wars would rage on until 1850, long after Napoleon Bonaparte had died. But perhaps more importantly, the crisis and the turmoil that resulted from the Peninsular War, gave rise to revolutions and fights for independence in much of South America, through which long centuries of Spanish rule were finally brought to an end. It was war - war all around.

Chapter VI
Napoleon Stands His Ground
War of the Fifth Coalition, April-October 1809

EVER SINCE THEIR BRUTAL downfall at the Battle of Austerlitz, the Austrians sought a way to avenge themselves on the French and regain the territories lost after the Treaty of Pressburg. Seeking the catalyst for another confrontation, they saw that the developing Peninsular War could be exploited against France. This became especially clear after the French defeat at Bailen, with Napoleon's reputation shaken. Nevertheless, Austria could never challenge France on its own - it desperately needed allies. But its ally of the previous wars, Russia, was now under a shaky peace with Napoleon, ever since the Treaty of Tilsit. Sweden too was unable to enter to its side, having been engaged in a conflict with Russia, especially when Finland was in question. One possible ally came to be the weakened Prussia, with some of its representatives wanting to help Austria. However, these hopes were soon dashed by the Convention of September 1808. Nevertheless, the Austrians eventually agreed to go to war, bolstered by the British involvement in Iberia, and the course of the war there. On February 8th, 1809, the Austrian advocates for war rejoiced as the Imperial Government opted for war.

But one thing that could have been better for the Austrians was the state of their army. After the crushing loss at Austerlitz, everything pointed to the fact that their army was in dire need of reformation.

After losing so many seasoned officers and veteran soldiers, and regular troops too, it was simply unable to refill those ranks in the regular method. Thus they relied on the *French* method of conscription, the so-called *Levée en masse,* which utilized mass national conscriptions. This resulted in the bulk of their army in the War of the Fifth Coalition to be inexperienced and lacking proper training. Oddly enough, this was the complete reversal of roles from the previous war - now it was the French that abandoned the mass national conscription, and instead relied on a regular army with seasoned soldiers. What this meant was that in this new conflict against Napoleon, Austrians would throw an army of raw recruits against the battle hardened veterans of the French. Talk about a bad idea.

Archduke Charles, the son of the Austrian Emperor, was the key figure for the Austrians in this war. When discussing the approach with which to face Napoleon, Charles and the Aulic Council came to their first divide. What Archduke Charles envisioned was a logical approach: to make a major push from the direction of Bohemia and aim to isolate the French troops that were stationed in the north of Germany, thus quickly deciding the outcome of the war. And with a good deal of the Austrian army already there, it seemed like a natural course to take. However, the Aulic Council wanted a different approach: if Charles' plan was adopted, they feared that the Danube river would become a critical separation of the Austrian forces. What they presented was a plan to launch an attack south of the Danube River and thus keep safe communications and supply lines with Vienna. And this was the plan chosen in the end. Napoleon on the other hand, lacked important information about the Austrians. When the latter declared war on him, he was freshly returning to Paris. He spent the winter of 1808-1809 in Spain, and was now having to face the Austrians. He realized that this new conflict was opening a second front for the French Empire, something with which he had to deal swiftly. He had some rough ideas about the Austiran operations, and instructed his main field commander in Germany, Berthier, to conduct deployments in order to react to the new front. Napoleon once more relied on his strategy from 1805, making the Danube valley the focus of his operations, without having any considerable knowledge about Austrian preparations. All of this contributed to rather poor deployments by the French army in the early stages of the War of the Fifth Coalition. But nevertheless, the fact that the conflict placed the raw recruits of the Austrians against the seasoned veterans of Napoleon meant that the latter still had an upper hand, even though lacking situational awareness. This turned the war into one of the shortest episodes of the Napoleonic Wars, lasting roughly 6 months. But even so, it was the last conflict from which Napoleon emerged as the decisive and triumphant winner.

Early engagements of the war began on April 10th 1809, when the Austrian army made the first move by crossing the River Inn in order to invade France's ally, Bavaria. Even though the bad conditions made Austrian advance slow, the Bavarians nonetheless retreated. These opening stages were not met adequately by the French. Napoleon misjudged the Austrians and expected their attack to come a week later than it did. This fact left Marshal Berthier in command. However, the latter was not able to deal with the situation adequately, mostly due to his lack of experience as a field commander. Moreover, a number of orders and messages from Paris were delayed. When they did arrive to Berthier, they were largely misinterpreted. All of this left the French Great Army of Germany in an unfavorable position, with two main wings separated by a 75 mile gap. On April 16th, Austrians exploited the thin Bavarian lines and defeated them at Landshut, thus securing a favorable crossing across the river Isar. This caused great frustration with Napoleon. He promptly arrived from Paris on the next day and was furious. Meanwhile, Archduke Charles was elated at the successful opening of the war. He next planned to utilize the twin pincer movement in order to defeat Marshal Davouts and Lefebvre's armies.

Seeing that the Austrians were already over the critical point - the Isar River - Napoleon furiously ordered that the entirety of his troops were to be deployed beyond the River Ilm in the protective square formation - within 48 hours. However, he made another misjudgement - where he thought that the Austrians had only a single corps en-route towards Davout in Regensburg, they had in fact a whole of five corps, totalling close to 80,000 men. This was a situation with possible catastrophic consequences, and Napoleon's left flank could be destroyed. Luckily, Marshal Davout, being the seasoned commander he was, anticipated the problems and pulled back his troops out of Regensburg where Berthier mistakenly placed him. Still commanding over the seasoned III Corps, Davout stumbled upon forward Austrian formations as he was heading north towards Neustadt. The Austrians were slow to react, and were easily repulsed by Davout.

The complex maneuvers and relocations that followed as Archduke Charles attempted to counter a shrewd southern maneuver by Napoleon eventually led to the first major battle of the War of the Fifth Coalition, the Battle of Aspern-Essling on May 21st. And it was this battle that would become the sobering call for Napoleon and his marshals. The initial stages of this battle were marked by disorganized and slow Austrian attacks against the village of Aspern. These attacks were a complete failure, but Archduke Charles was not dismayed. The small town of Essling saw even fiercer street fighting that led to many casualties on both sides. The fighting continued on the next day as well, and found the Frenchmen badly outnumbered. Napoleon thus launched a critical and large scale attack against the Austrian center, hoping to buy enough time for Davout's III Corps to cross the river and secure a victory. Marshal Jean Lannes was the one to advance with 3 divisions, but was repulsed by devastating Austrian fire. Charles then ordered a massive attack which claimed Aspern, and eventually Essling as well. However, Napoleon ordered his General Jean Rapp to send only a part of his troops in, but the latter disobeyed his direct orders and attacked with full force and retook Essling from the Austrians. The latter then proceeded to bombard the town with absolutely devastating and concentrated cannon fire. Napoleon eventually pulled his forces out of the battle, suffering the first major defeat in over a decade. The Battle of Aspern-Essling was a catastrophe in many regards. The bombardment of Essling claimed many lives. One of those was the life of the French General Pouzet. His head was blown off by a cannon ball as he was conversing face to face with his old friend Marshal Jean Lannes. The latter was utterly shocked, and went to compose himself beside a ditch, sitting with his legs crossed and catching a breath. A recoiling cannon ball struck his legs, wounding him badly. After an amputation, Marshal Lannes - Napoleon's personal friend and one of his best commanders - died several days later.

Another victim of this battle was the famed General Saint-Hillaire, another of Napoleon's key commanders. His left leg was torn off by a cannon ball at Essling. He too died 15 days later.

Napoleon was clearly taken aback by the defeat at Aspern-Essling, made even worse by the loss of his dear friend and competent commander, Lannes. It took him six weeks of recuperation and planning, before making another attempt to cross the Danube. However, it is important to note that the Austrians failed to capitalize on their victory, and thus gave Napoleon the preparation time and incentive to continue his attack. He managed to reinforce his troops, bring in more cannons and maintain his supply lines. And for any capable commander - and who more capable than Napoleon - that was all that was needed to secure victory. And Napoleon secured it at the crucial Battle of Wagram.

Starting on July 30th, 1809, the French army - roughly 188,000 strong - crossed over the danube and began its march towards the Austrians. The latter were stationed around the village of Wagram.

Napoleon's attacks were vicious from the get-go. He ordered his troops to commence an attack along the entirety of the Austrian lines, as to prevent their hasty escape. Initial assaults proved to be almost decisive, however the Austrians managed to hold their positions. The continued Austrian perseverance meant that the first day of the fighting was costly in casualties for both sides, but produced no results.

However, on the next day, Austrian Archduke Charles planned a critical "double-envelopment" approach, but its results were mixed: the French right side held out easily, but the left was almost destroyed. All the while, Bernadotte made a shocking order over the course of night, by ordering his troops out of the crucial French position at the central village of Aderklaa. He thus dangerously compromised the French positions in the battle. Upon hearing this, Napoleon was furiously angry, immediately sending two division and cavalry support to regain that position. Aderklaa changed hands twice, with heavy loss of life.

The Battle of Wagram turned out into a vicious, prolonged engagement that saw repetitive advanced by the French repulsed under a rain of deadly cannon barrage. However, when three French divisions at last managed to penetrate the Austrian lines after an all-out offensive, the Archduke Charles realized that his positions were at a breaking point. He thus ordered a complete retreat from the battle, leaving Napoleon victorious. However, the victory came at a cost - both sides suffered close to 40,000 casualties each: a catastrophic loss of life.

Soon after Wagram, the Fifth Coalition effectively ended, and it's War was once more a victory for Napoleon. Archduke Charles promptly signed an armistice after the battle, even though his army was not entirely decimated. The aftermath of the war was the signing of the Treaty of Schönbrunn on October 14th, 1809, which was a heavy diplomatic defeat for the Austrians. They had to cede a great majority of their territories to the French, and were thus immensely weakened as a power. Through these territorial losses, Austria also lost roughly three million of its subjects, transferring them into Napoleon's hands.

Chapter VII
The War Across the Water
War of 1812

WHEN WE DISCUSS THE Napoleonic Wars as a broader historical period, it is inevitable that we will have to eventually reach upon numerous conflicts that branched out from this critically tumultuous period in the world's history. While the *War of 1812* is considered by American historians as a conflict largely separated from the Napoleonic Wars, British and European historians regard it as its integral part. The Napoleonic Wars were without a doubt a *global* conflict, and the impact it made reached many corners of the world. The United States was one such theater.

The United States of America gained independence in 1776 - relatively recently in comparison to the start of the Napoleonic Wars. However, a greater part of its young history as a nation was spent in a state of war, even before independence was gained. The North American continent was still a land rife with indigenous tribes, and conflict emerged at every step. But the War of 1812 was the first serious conflict for this young nation, and truly brought it onto the great global stage. This conflict pitted it against the British, and was waged across the American Northeast, Midwest, and Southeast, as well across Canada and its Great Lakes region. In fact, Canada - which was then under British rule - would become the central battleground of this war.

The precursor to the War of 1812 was without a doubt the greater Napoleonic conflict. Since its beginning, Napoleon and the British were in a fierce economic duel, seeking to cripple one another by restricting international trade. This was made all the more worse with the French Continental System. The United States were a significant source of income for all European nations, and a major trading partner. However, with the conflict between France and Britain raging in earnest, the United States were placed in a no-solution situation: they could not effectively trade with either of these two major powers, without risking to anger them. They were thus sinking into an increasing economic depression. Seeking a solution, the States contested the British naval blockades as illegal under the international law. Another thing that caused discord between these two powers were the twelve "Orders in Council", which the British Parliament issued between 1783 and 1812. These orders declared that any merchant ship headed for French ports could be searched and seized. Britain also dismissed the American declaration of neutrality in the Napoleonic Wars, essentially ignoring it as an independent nation. Moreover, there was plenty of tension between the Americans and the British: the latter continued to supply weapons to the Native American tribes, much to the dismay of frontier settlers, and there were also several naval incidents that provoked conflict. After much debate in the American Congress, with plenty of advocates for war, the then President, James Madison, signed the declaration of war on June 18th 1812. The declaration was largely instigated by the so-called "war hawks" in the American congress, and was the first formal declaration of war in the history of this nation. With the memories of the American Revolution still fresh, many Americans hailed this declaration of war as the "Second War of Independence".

One interesting factor ensued after the declaration. The British chose to repeal the trade restrictions even before learning of the war. Since the formal declaration of war had to travel by sea from North America to Britain - a journey that took almost a month and a half by ship - it reached Britain well after the trade restrictions were removed. However, with all the confusion ensuing from this, the war still proceeded. Now it was the fight of odds: The poorly trained American army fielded close to 7,000 men, compared to seasoned and well trained British Army which numbered more than 240,000 soldiers across the globe. Their fleet was equally smaller in comparison to the British Royal Navy. Nevertheless, there was the great expanse of water separating the two nations, and the Americans wanted to quickly bring the British to the negotiations table. This they planned to do by invading Canada and seizing its key territories. At the time, Canada was still a land full of wilderness and rich with resources. Seizing these territories could be a big blow for the British. However, the invasion of Canada ended in failure. The Americans lost their battles at the Siege of Detroit and the costly Battle of Queenston Heights on the Niagara river, all the while having to suffer raids and massacres from Native American tribes allied to the British. In 1813, some success was gained by the Americans - the Battle of Lake Erie was won, allowing them to capture Detroit and go on to defeat the Native American confederation led by Tecumseh.

But at the sea the Americans fared somewhat better. Even as the British Royal Navy maintained partial dominance by creating a semi-tight naval blockade all along the Atlantic seaboard, the outnumbered American ships managed to win a few decisive clashes and battles. Throughout the War of 1812, the American navy managed to put up a fight against the British at sea.

In 1813, a key event occurred, known as the *River Raisin Massacre.* After the Battle of Frenchtown, which pitted outnumbered and inexperienced Kentucky recruits against a larger force of British and their Native American Potawatomi allies, the former chose to surrender. The British ensured them of their safety, but the Native Americans later massacred a great number of wounded and straggling men. The massacre caused great anger across America, especially in Kentucky, where many recruits volunteered to war seeking vengeance.

In the second part of 1813, the Americans once more failed to capture Montreal and gain a foothold in Canada, after suffering two defeats, at the Battle of Chateauguay, and the Battle of Crysler's Farm.

One significant victory however, occurred in September 1813, when the American naval commander, Oliver Hazard Perry won a major victory at Lake Erie.

By the end of 1813, a conflict erupted amongst the Native American Creek tribes. They descended into an all-out war between opposing factions: some wanted to retain their traditional ways of life, influenced by the late leader Tecumseh, while the other wanted to adopt the culture of the Americans. Those opposed to the modern way of life became known as the "Red Sticks" faction, and began increasingly attacking American outposts and forts. In the winter of 1813-1814, Andrew Jackson would organize a crucial militia force that would go on to defeat the *Red Sticks* at the major Battle of Horseshoe Bend in 1814, which effectively ended the conflict with the Creek Indians. This victory resulted in the all-important Treaty of Fort Jackson, through which the Creek Indians were forced to cede roughly 23 *million* acres of land - all of which would eventually become parts of Georgia and Alabama.

New changes also began appearing in 1814 - the influential Brigadier General Winfield Scott began implementing a new plan of *strict drill* for all the American troops on the Canadian border. It was these very troops that would advance into Upper Canada and manage to achieve a decisive victory at the Battle of Chippawa in July of that year. However, they suffered a defeat weeks later, at Battle of Lundy's Lane.

By the time of Napoleon's first exile, and the short-term peace in Europe, the British could divert more troops and resources to North America. This greatly shifted the tone of the war up to that point, and placed great pressures on the Americans. It was at this period that the Secretary of the Treasury, Albert Gallatin, famously said: "*Hereafter we should have to fight not for "free trade and the rights of sailors", nor for the conquest of the Canadas - but for our own national existence".*

By August 1814, the British sent an expeditionary force of roughly 4,500 seasoned veterans commanded by General Robert Ross. They landed in Maryland and at once began their dazzlingly fast campaign. They promptly defeated the Maryland militia in the Battle of Bladensburg, and proceeded to capture and burn public institutions in Washington DC, including the White House and the Capitol. This was a huge demoralizing blow for the Americans.

Robert Ross, a seasoned veteran commander of the European theater, proceeded to attack Baltimore, without success. The Maryland militia managed to hold their ground during the Battle of the North Point. Ross was shot and killed during these skirmishes.

Nevertheless, on the 24th of December, 1814, the Treaty of Ghent - a bilateral peace treaty - was signed between America and Britain, bringing peace. However, the word of that peace was once more slow to travel across the water, and that resulted in the Battle of New Orleans on January 8th 1815, where Andrew Jackson won a decisive victory for the Americans - oblivious of the peace agreement. Luckily, the peace was officially declared by President Madison on February 18th, 1815, bringing the War of 1812 to a long desired end. It was popularly stated that the United States of America greeted this peace treaty not with "a shout of triumph" but with a "sigh of relief". The War of 1812 claimed 15,000 American lives, at the time a big loss for this still young nation.

The terms in the Treaty of Ghent were the so-called *status quo antebellum:* a reversal to the state as it was before the war. All land was returned to its original owners. As such the War of 1812 was a draw, and in many regards a *pointless* loss of life and resources. Nevertheless, the British lifted their trade restrictions and impressment policies, and also stopped supplying Native American tribes with weapons and gunpowder. This last point was a big blow for the Native American tribes. Many of them fought in the War on the British side, hoping for a recognition of a Native Nation in North America. This however, was promptly dismissed by the British, and the Indian sacrifice was in vain. What is more, without the British-supplied weapons and money, the Native tribes had no chance to defend their territories or raid the new American settlers. This led to increased American expansion and the rapid dwindling of the Indians.

After the War of 1812, the American society experienced a few years of general prosperity. The world peace bolstered a hasty economic revival, and the politics of the United States were developing. However, only a few decades later, the American Civil War will once again plunge the continent into bitter and vicious war.

Chapter VIII
The Bitter Taste of Failure
French Invasion of Russia, June-
December 1812

AS THE WAR OVER THE seas was beginning in 1812, so it did resume in Europe. With a majority of Western and Central European nations under the flag of Napoleon's vast French Empire - both directly and indirectly - there was still a large threat to all of his possessions: *Russia*. The Peninsular War on the Iberian Peninsula has already boiled over, and by 1812 was a complex and costly conflict for France. In fact, it was becoming a thorn in Napoleon's side, exacting a great toll on the economy of France, on the morale of his troops, and the wavering political support in his realm. This was an almost secret aspect: the French Empire appeared to be at its greatest heights of power in 1811, but that was in fact merely a facade - it was on a steady decline. Napoleon himself was becoming overweight by 1812, and was prone to various aches and ailments. And the conflict with Russia was about to become one of the greatest tests in Napoleon's life.

One of the main precursors to this conflict was the Treaty of Schönbrunn, of which we already wrote. It was the treaty that came after the end of the last major conflict, between Austria and France in 1800. That treaty had one peculiar clause: it removed the territory of *Western Galicia* from Austria, and annexed it to the Grand Duchy of Warsaw, the French client state created by Napoleon. It is key to emphasize here that Poland and the neighboring regions of modern-day Ukraine were ever a contention point between Russia and West European powers, chiefly Poland. The same occurred in this case, as Russia's Emperor saw this annexed territory as a viable position for future invasions of Russia. And, indeed, its location was such as to threaten the borders of the Russian Empire. Thus, in 1811, the Russian command set to develop a strategic plan for a possible offensive war, through which they would attack Warsaw and Danzig.

Another precursor for war was the Russian withdrawal from Napoleon's flawed Continental System. They found that their economy was losing immensely due to it, as Russia was a land incredibly rich with raw resources, but with limited manufacture, and thus greatly depended on export and import. When they chose to withdraw from Napoleon's system, tensions escalated even further, giving France the incentive to go to war. Again the economy placed a crucial role in instigating war. By attacking Russia - and hopefully defeating it - Napoleon hoped to force the Russian Tsar to stop his trade with Britain and force a peace. When the Russians began amassing troops on their borders after the situation in Poland, Napoleon famously asked the Russian ambassador in Vienna, Prince Alexander Kurakin: *"What does this mean? What does Russia want from me? You know it's easy to start a war but it's very difficult to finish one."*

Before the war erupted, Napoleon made an attempt to gain support from the Polish people, relying on their age-old tensions with the Russians. Thus he called the war with Russia "the Second Polish War", reflecting on the so-called First Polish War, another name for the War of the Fourth Coalition in 1806-08. It was what the Polish patriots wanted to hear: their desire was to reclaim the Russian part of Poland and to see a re-establishment of an independent Poland. However, Napoleon knew that this would never happen - Austria was guaranteed that the idea of an independent Poland would never come to fruition.

After a prolonged period of setting up the logistics, Napoleon at last commenced his campaign to invade Russia and achieve his plans. He wanted to trap and destroy the Russian army - or the bulk of it - somewhere on the frontier near or at the city of Smolensk. Following this, he intended to fortify both strategic towns of Smolensk and Minsk, make there his winter quarters, and wait until spring and either continue the war or accept peace. For his "Russian campaign" Napoleon amassed the largest army ever assembled up to that point in European history: a force of roughly 685,000 men. Opposing them was a lesser - but no less immense - force of roughly 488,000 Russian troops.

Before the start of his campaign, Napoleon ignored the repeated advice against the invasion, and it at last commenced on June 24th, 1812, with the French Great Army crossing the River Niemen. Just before he began, Napoleon sent one last offer of peace to St. Petersburg, but received no reply. From this point on, history was to be made, and Napoleon knew it when he said famously: *"Let Destiny be accomplished".* His initial progress was swift - through a series of long and well organized marches, his Grande Armee moved rapidly through Russia. Along the way, the French won several minor skirmishes and battles, until the first major clash - the Battle of Smolensk in mid August 1812. This battle resulted in a decisive French victory, and left the city of Smolensk almost entirely burned to the ground. This was not according to Napoleon's plan, as it denied him a strategic supply base he wanted as well as his winter quarters. In the meanwhile, the Russian army was on a constant retreat further inland for almost three whole months, and adopted a "scorched earth" tactic to deny Napoleon the supplies he needed and cause immense logistical issues. Entire towns, villages, and vast fields of crops were burned to ash by mobile *Cossack* cavalry units, denying Napoleon the option of living off the land.

However, this Russian tactic was not met with acceptance amongst the ranks of the Russian nobility. The latter depended on their vast territories. At the time, Russia had a lot of noble Princes and Counts, who all relied on a system of *serfdom*, owning peasants, villages, and land. By adopting the scorched earth tactic, the commander of the Russian army, Field Marshal Barclay de Tolly was greatly upsetting them. Finally, the nobles pressured Emperor Alexander to relieve Tolly of his duty, and he replaced him with the old, but able veteran commander Prince Mikhail Kutuzov. Kutuzov too kept on the retreat following the defeat at Smolensk, but as both armies were approaching Moscow, he opted for fighting rather than letting it fall to the French. He thus took up defensive positions some 120 kilometers (~75 miles) outside of Moscow, close to *Borodino*.

The Battle of Borodino thus began on September 7th, 1812, as the French army caught up with the Russians. It would become one of the bloodiest, most vicious single-day battles of the Napoleonic Wars, and military history as a whole. The battle involved roughly 250,000 men and left 68,000 dead, in just the single day of fighting. Borodino was immortalized in detail by the great writer Leo Tolstoy, in his work "War and Peace". This critical engagement was a turning point of the campaign, and saw the French army attacking the semi-fortified positions of the Russians under Kutuzov. The battle was notorious for its ferocity, and an all out skirmish that became a chaotic, hand to hand bloodshed. Napoleon eventually managed to secure the central parts of the battlefield, most notably the so-called "Bagration fleches", in which the famous Russian General Pyotr Bagration lost his life. However, even after winning, Napoleon did not manage to destroy the Russian army as he envisioned. The latter could easily replenish their troops on their own territory, while Napoleon could not.

Borodino was unique in many aspects. It was one of the most vicious of all Napoleonic battles, and as such it placed a great toll on the troops on the field. The battle was concluded with a French *tactical* victory, and saw the Russians retreating while still offering resistance. However, Napoleon did not pursue as he had done before. Many historians argue that Napoleon made one singular and crucial mistake at Borodino, which ultimately cost him the campaign: he refused to commit his heavy Imperial Guard to the battle, which remained in position and was not engaged throughout. With it, he could have turned the tide of the battle at any time. He believed that the battle could be decided without the intervention of the Imperial Guard, which was his most valuable unit. If committed, it would have been greatly weakened. All of his key Marshals advised him to do so, including Rapp, Ney, and Murat - but he still refused. So, even though he won, the Russian army was not destroyed and could flee in combat strength.

On the next day, the Russian army was virtually halved, and Kutuzov retreated beyond Moscow, completely evacuating the city. Nevertheless, through massive recruitments and reinforcements, the Russian forces would steadily be filled back up to strength. The rearguards of the Russian army continued to give battle to Napoleon immediately after Borodino, harrying his advance, as the Russian retreat changed course towards the south instead of the east. These rear guard actions were led by the Serbian-Russian General Mikhail Miloradovich, one of the most prominent figures of the period. By persisting in delaying actions, he allowed for a full evacuation of Moscow before finally retreating around September 14th. On that very same day, Napoleon reached the Russian capital of Moscow with his army. However, to his surprise, no one was there to either surrender or resist. What he encountered was a city completely deserted. Moscow's governor, Count Rostopchin, completely stripped the town of all valuables and supplies, and also ordered for the city's prisons to be opened. Those few that remained in the town - prisoners included - resorted to looting and burning of what little remained. On that first night of the French occupation of Moscow, a fire broke out in the bazaar and soon spread throughout the city. Moscow at the time had a majority of wooden buildings, and soon enough, roughly four fifths of the entire town was reduced to ash. This was a deliberate action by Count Rostopchin who left orders for the town to be set ablaze. All efforts of the French to contain the fires were in vain.

Seeing the destruction of Moscow, and realizing that the Russians were not going to surrender, Napoleon found himself in a difficult situation. His supplies were low, his troops idle, and winter steadily approaching. He had no choice but to retreat, leaving Moscow in mid October 1812.

He made another attempt at engaging the Russians at the Battle of Maloyaroslavets, but could not destroy them, and was eventually forced back onto the road towards Smolensk from whence he came. In years past, Napoleon and his Grande Armee developed a habit of relying on the land for their supplies, which was made all the easier in central Europe with its developed agriculture and network of roads. However, with the Russians burning their crops, the French were left with nothing but devastated earth. In the following weeks, as the French army retreated in the grip of a particularly harsh winter, it was reduced to a shambling skeleton of the giant that came marching into Russia just a few months before. Resupplying was impossible, food was lacking, as did the winter clothes. The horses had no forage nor grass to graze on, and were steadily killed for food by the starving French troops. This destroyed the proud French cavalry, which was reduced to mere foot soldiers. What is more, without the horses, the French had to abandon their cannons and wagons. Starvation and biting cold led to hypothermia, death and disease, and many French soldiers deserted - only to be killed by the Russian peasants. Moreover, the Cossack cavalry continually harassed the French rear, inflicting further casualties. All in all, the French retreat from Russia was an absolute and utter disaster, and one of the greatest trials up to that point. More French soldiers died from suicide, disease, cold, and starvation, than in all the battles of the campaign combined. This disaster culminated with the Battle of the Berezina River, as two Russian armies descended on the ragged remnants of the Grande Armee as it tried to flee across the river crossings. It was the final massacre of the French - they eventually left Russian soil in mid December 1812, bringing this disastrous campaign to an end.

The failed Russian campaign cost Napoleon dearly. The casualties amounted to roughly 200,000 dead and close to 190,000 captured, which decimated his army by more than a half. The campaign became one of the most lethal and costly military operations in world's history. Similar mistakes would be repeated many, many decades later, when Hitler attempted the invasion of Russia and met almost the identical fate as Napoleon. Needless to say, Napoleon's reputation was shaken to the core - if not shattered. The French domination in Europe was put to the test and significantly weakened. As such, the failure of this campaign was the crucial trigger for a major shift in European politics and the flow of the Napoleonic Wars. Hoping to exploit the weakened Napoleon, both Prussia and Austria broke their *imposed* alliances and switched sides, heralding the start of the War of the Sixth Coalition.

Chapter IX
The Downfall
War of the Sixth Coalition, March 1813 - May 1814

THERE WAS ONLY A SHORT amount of time for both Napoleon and his enemies to recuperate from the devastation of the winter campaign and try to strengthen their numbers. Arguably, it was a far greater challenge for the French, whose numbers were so fiercely decimated in that catastrophic endeavor. But Napoleon's enemies were not wasting time, and soon enough a new, Sixth Coalition against France was formed. It was bound to ensure Napoleon's downfall, but he was determined not to go down without a fight. He managed to bring his troop numbers back up in a surprising amount of time, bolstering his numbers in the east from 30,000 to 130,000, and eventually bringing the total numbers of troops in Germany to roughly 400,000. Granted, he needed to utilize a good deal of fresh recruits in order to do this.

By March 1813, the Sixth Coalition was steadily progressing. After Napoleon's failure in Russia, both Prussia and Austria switched sides, with the latter assuming the position of armed neutrality. Sweden also entered into this coalition against France, allying itself with the United Kingdom and promptly liberating the so-called Swedish Pomerania. On March 17th, the Prussian King Frederick III declared war on France and called his people to arms. Prussia seemed eager to once more descend into conflict with Napoleon, and the first minor battle soon occurred at Möckern, where the Prussians won.

As he was seeking solutions to reinforce his numbers in Central Europe - where the majority of the conflict was to be - Napoleon had to withdraw roughly 20,000 seasoned troops from the Iberian Peninsula, thus weakening France's effort in the ongoing Peninsular War. This proved to be a major weakening, as Napoleon's brother, Joseph Bonaparte soon had to abandon Madrid as the Duke of Wellington decisively defeated the French repeatedly across Spain. He took Burgos in May, won the Battle of Vitoria in late June, and defeated Marshal Soult in late July in the Battle of the Pyrenees, which brought him to the doorstep of the French. This would be crucial in the later developments of the War of the Sixth Coalition.

In the initial months of the war, Austria attempted to remain loyal to France - its foreign minister Metternich wanted to mediate a peace between France and the forces of the Coalition, but this could only be possible under the terms that Napoleon would never agree to.

The first battles soon began. Although lasting just little over a year, the War of the Sixth Coalition would be filled with critical engagements, and with battles both large and small, with heavy cost of life. On May 2nd 1813, the Battle of Lützen saw Napoleon halting the advances of the Coalition, albeit at a high cost of life. Since he lacked cavalry after his Russian campaign, Napoleon was unable to pursue the retreating enemy, and thus capitalize on his victory as he used to do. This situation would go on to repeat itself throughout the War of the Sixth Coalition, essentially robbing Napoleon of decisive results.

Soon after, on May 20th, Napoleon won another costly battle at Bautzen with similar results.

Nevertheless, even though he lost a roughly equal number of man as the Coalition forces, Napoleon's initial victories worked to greatly lower the morale of Russians and Prussians. Both these armies suffered immense losses in the opening stages of the war, and now it was becoming obvious that such losses will be difficult to fill. In essence, both were utterly decimated. Moreover, a large number of high-up officers of the Russian army began expressing the desire to return to Russia, since their original goal of forcing Napoleon out of their country was successful. King of Prussia, Frederick III was also expressing certain doubts about the new war with Napoleon, having had his nose bloodied at Bautzen and Lützen, after urging his folk to rise to war so fervently just months before. Now, the only hope for both Russians and Prussians was the involvement of Austria, which up to that point was not engaged in action.

However, Napoleon was in dire straits. His army was now majority fresh recruits and was in desperate need of many crucial resources - many of which were in short supply after the Russian fiasco. The new conscripts were also less hardy than the seasoned veterans - they quickly got exhausted from Napoleon's notorious long, forced marches and constant maneuvering. All of this meant that the French army was in desperate need of a period of peace in which to resupply, recover, and reorganize. Not to mention the fact that Napoleon was almost without horses, and these had to be acquired again. So, when the coalition forces offered an armistice, Napoleon was amiable to it. However, this short armistice was soon to end, especially after Napoleon had a disastrous interview with the Austrian chancellor Metternich, in which a fierce argument ensued. When the war got underway, Napoleon would quickly realize that relying on the armistice was a mistake - the Coalition forces gained so much more out of it than he did. In the end, Austria entered the Sixth Coalition and declared war on France formally in August 1813.

The armistice lasted from June 4th 1813 to August 13th of that same year, and gave just a short respite to both sides. After it ended, the Coalition forces were greatly bolstered by the newly included Austrian forces. The latter brought roughly 300,000 soldiers into the fray, bringing the total number of Coalition troops to roughly 800,000 frontline troops and 350,000 soldiers in reserve. This proved Napoleon's mistake, as he now lost the numerical advantage and thus the initiative in the war that he originally had.

After the armistice, the battles soon resumed again. Napoleon gained a decisive victory at the Battle of Dresden between 26th and 27th August 1813, where he decimated the combined Prussian, Austrian, and Russian army. In this battle, Napoleon arrived in the nick of time to reinforce the attacked French garrison in Dresden. Outnumbered, he still risked an attack, succeeding at pining his enemy at the Weißeritz River. This gave the cuirassiers and lancers of Joachim Murat a clear chance, which they exploited and thus shredded the trapped enemy to pieces, winning the battle through savage bloodshed. But even with this victory, the unfavorable weather did not allow Napoleon to capitalize and fulfill his plan of encircling the Coalition forces. The Battle of Dresden was one of the last chances Napoleon had to end the War of the Sixth Coalition in a single day - but he could not seize that chance.

In the meantime, as Napoleon marched with the majority of his force towards Dresden, the Prussian army under the command of Count Von Blücher took the advantage and attacked the forces of the French Marshal MacDonald at the Battle of Katzbach. It took place on the very same day as the Battle of Dresden, and all under the terrible downpour of rain. Here, the Prussians won the day, forcing the French army to retreat towards Saxony. Katzbach was a terrible loss for the French: they suffered 13,000 casualties and 20,000 captured, compared to only 4,000 casualties on the Prussian side.

On September 6th 1813, the French suffered another terrible defeat, this time at the hands of a combined Prussian and Swedish army. It occured when Napoleon was attempting to capture Berlin, believing that doing so would force Prussia out of the war. He left his Marshal Ney in command at Dennewitz, but Ney fell into a trap set up by the Swedes, suffering terrible casualties and a crushing defeat. With

20,000 casualties suffered, this defeat was a disaster for Napoleon. Not only did he lose the chance to seize Berlin, but also the initiative for good this time. Now he was forced to seek a decisive battle and put all of his cards on the table. And that was the Battle of Leipzig.

He withdrew a 175,000 men strong army to Leipzig in Saxon. Here he hoped to fight a defensive battle against the combined Coalition armies - but on his own terms. This became the Battle of Nations (or the Battle of Leipzig), that was fought between 16th and 19th October 1813. The French army numbered close to 190,000 troops after receiving reinforcements, and was facing a massive force of more than 430,000 Coalition troops converging on Napoleon. The Battle of the Nations was the largest battle ever fought in Europe, until the beginning of the First World War. It was a vicious, bloody battle and one of the greatest losses of life in the Napoleonic Wars, with more than 127,000 combined casualties. Leipzig was another, crucial defeat of Napoleon. He was forced to a retreat, leaving Marshal Jozef Poniatowski to cover his retreat. The latter died doing so, and the Coalition forces eventually captured 30,000 French troops after they were left stranded. Napoleon retreated to France with the remnants of his army.

Following their victory at Leipzig, the Coalition forces offered Napoleon peace in November 1813. The terms of this peace were as follows: Napoleon gets to keep his title as Emperor of France, but the later gets "reset" to its natural frontiers - i.e. he loses all his conquered territories. The Austrian chancellor Metternich told Napoleon that these were by far the best terms that the Coalition forces would ever offer him. And he certainly was correct - the terms were more than generous. However, driven by his ambition and hope, Napoleon still believed he could win the war and thus delayed with making his decision. After a while, the Coalition withdrew the peace offer, continuing the war.

Meanwhile, as Napoleon was retreating into France, the British forces under the Duke of Wellington were exploiting the situation and rushing in from the Iberian Peninsula. Wellington led his *Peninsular Army* across the Pyrenees Mountain, gaining victories at the Battles of Nive, Nivelle, and Vera pass, as well as the Battles of Orthez and Toulouse, entering well into France by April 1814.

On the other hand, Napoleon still fought on. In his retreat, he fought a series of defensive battles within France, most notably the Battle of Arcis-sur-Aube, but without any gains. His zeal and devotion to his vision were now bordering the impossible: in France he issued an order for 900,000 fresh recruits - a stellar number. Only a fraction of this number was ever recruited. Napoleon was growing increasingly outnumbered, commanding only around 80,000 troops in February 1814, after leading a Six Days' Campaign in which he won a series of battles against a numerically superior enemy. Nevertheless, the Coalition forces still had roughly 400,000 men at their disposal.

It was becoming clear that Napoleon's days were numbered - his downfall was beginning. Knowing this, the powers of the Coalition signed the Treaty of Chaumont on March 9th 1814, vowing to keep up the fight until Napoleon was totally defeated. Soon after, they brought the fight to the streets of Paris. Between March 30th and 31st, Napoleon led the defense of his capital at the Battle of Paris. He failed, and the Coalition forces won a decisive victory.

Napoleon's surrender was now a certainty. The Russian Emperor triumphantly entered Paris, sending envoys to accept his enemy's surrender. He was given the keys of the city by the French Minister of Foreign Affairs, Talleyrand, on March 31st. However, still blindly devoted, Napoleon wanted to fight on and retake Paris. But his senior officers and Marshals saw the futility in this, and collectively mutinied. They approached Napoleon on April 4th, expressing their refusal to obey. Marshal Ney was at their head. Two days before that, the French Senate passed an act that officially deposed Napoleon, much to the latter's fury. Seeing that he was given no choice, and being abandoned by his Marshals, Napoleon abdicated unconditionally on April 6th, 1814. One of the terms of his abdication was also his exile to the Island of Elba. This was a complex couple of days with numerous intricate events unfolding. Nevertheless, the War of the Sixth Coalition was at last over, and - as many thought - the Napoleonic Wars were over too. However, Napoleon had other plans...

Chapter X
The Final Dare
War of the Seventh Coalition, 20 March – 8 July 1815

AFTER NAPOLEON'S DEFEAT and exile to the little Island of Elba, located some 10 kilometers from the Italian mainland, things in France were far from ideal. The Bourbon dynasty was restored to the French throne in the Bourbon Restoration, almost immediately after Napoleon was exiled. However, the latter spent only 9 months in his not-so-remote exile, patiently watching the unfolding events and hatching a plan for his return to power. Barely in touch with Paris, Napoleon scrounged every bit of information he could get to assert the situation in France as accurately as possible. And things were indeed unfolding in a way that he could predict - the dissolution of his Empire and the return to the old borders of Royal France was far, far from ideal, and caused a wave of dissatisfaction amongst the common folk. The Bourbon princes and the returning nobility treated the people as bad as before, especially the veterans of Napoleon's Great Army, who certainly deserved better treatment. What is more, Europe as a whole was dangerously stressed and pressured, after years and years of almost constant warfare. All of this came as a crucial and generally favorable piece of news for Napoleon, who judged that the situation would dictate a favorable reaction from the French people if he were to return. Another factor that bolstered his ever-high hopes was the fact that - with the war supposedly over - the French prisoners of war would be returning en-masse to France, and could become a seasoned, veteran core of his new army. It was not too hard to spot all these favorable signs, and even Napoleon's enemies could see the situation. Thus many of them suggested that he should be deported to an even remoter location, such as the Azores Islands, or the distant Saint Helena. Some even wanted to assassinate him.

Meanwhile, the Allied powers gathered to convene at the all-important Congress of Vienna, which lasted from November 1814 to June 1815, and still remains as one of the most crucial political conferences in European history. However, the powers gathered had conflicting views and ideas for the future of Europe. So different, in fact, that they nearly went to war with one another. The proud Prussian King *demanded* the entirety of the Kingdom of Saxony for himself, while the Russian Emperor Alexander wanted to take as much of Poland as he could, leaving the Duchy of Warsaw in existence - to protect his own borders. Austria wanted the ever-contended Northern Italy, and would not allow the wishes of either Prussia or Russia to come to pass. The British supported the French and the Austrians. These conflicting goals led to an all-time high tension at the Congress, which almost led to a war, as the Russian Emperor "politely" pointed out that his Empire had 450,000 men on his borders and all were welcome to try and move them from there.

But, as that old proverb tells us, while the cat is asleep, the mice come out to play. Or better yet, when the mice are arguing, the old tomcat comes out on the prowl. And that old tomcat was Napoleon Bonaparte. He exploited the lengthy process of the Congress of Vienna, and managed to slip away from his exile on 26th of February 1815. He slipped on board a French ship with roughly a thousand supporters, and escaped from the Portoferraio port on Elba. By March 1st he landed on French soil, in the south. Right from the start, he was received with open arms, except in the royalist region of Provence. Gradually, day by day, he gathered those loyal to him, and as the troop numbers began to grow, Napoleon once more had the makings of an army at his disposal. Those troops that were supposed to be Royalist, were clearly still ardent supporters of their ex-Emperor, and began flocking to his side en-masse. At one incident, a regiment of Royalist troops were deployed to stop Napoleon's advance near Grenoble. Before the clash began, Napoleon himself stepped in front of the Royalist troops, unbuttoned his long coat and spread his arms, saying: *"If any one of you will shoot his Emperor, here I am."* All of the men went over to his side. Even his ex-Marshals began returning to Napoleon, creating the image of the state of things as they used to be. Marshal Michel Ney, nicknamed the "Bravest of the Brave", became a Royalist commander after Napoleon's exile. He also said that the latter ought to be brought to Paris in a cage. However, by March 14th 1815, he too joined Napoleon, bringing roughly 6,000 men to his side. Some five days later, bolstered and ambitious, Napoleon entered Paris once more, to the cheers of the gathered crowds. King Louis XVIII fled in panic. The Royalist forces in France were no match for Napoleon, nor his swelled numbers.

Soon after these events, both Napoleon, and the nations of the newly formed Seventh Coalition, began preparing for yet another new war. As Napoleon marched through France gathering his supporters, the Congress of Vienna was still underway. Hearing of his return, the major powers signed a declaration that declared him an *outlaw*, and officially began the War of the Seventh Coalition. All of these powers also vouched to deliver 150,000 troops to the war - each. Only Britain could not meet this demand.

But however devoted, zealous, ambitious, and hopeful Napoleon might have been, the numbers did not lie. And what the numbers said was not favorable. Returning to Paris, Napoleon discovered that Louis XVIII left him with little resources, making his situation all the more challenging. Nevertheless, he slowly amassed a sizable army of both seasoned veterans and raw recruits. By the end of May 1815 he had roughly 198,000 men at his disposal, with further 66,000 recruits in training. On the other hand, his enemies boasted an army of roughly 850,000 men, separated in four separate fronts. But even though he was badly outnumbered, Napoleon was no first-timer, and could choose the way this war would unfold, hoping to make the numbers work for him. He needed to decide on a good strategy and develop a plan, fighting either an offensive, or a defensive war. While one might expect that in his situation he would opt to defend his borders, fortifying key cities and leading a guerilla war, Napoleon actually opted to attack. He envisioned a pre-emptive strike before the Coalition forces were fully prepared and in connection with one another. With one critical victory, he could force the Seventh Coalition to sue for peace, which would be favorable for Napoleon. However, this time he found a bit of reason: through such peace he would want to remain at the head of France and not much more.

Napoleon's plan entailed an attack in Belgium. There were several reasons for this choice: he knew that the British and Prussian presence there was scattered and not fully organized; he learned that the British forces were mostly second-line troops; and a victory in Belgium could win over the French-speaking Brussels to his cause. And the campaign that emerged from the French attack in Belgium would prove to be the decisive conflict, and Napoleon's last.

Known as the Waterloo campaign, it lasted from June 15th to July 8th, 1815, and was fought between the French army and the combined armies of the British and the Prussians. Marshals Ney, Grouchy, Davout, and Soult were all involved alongside Napoleon, while the Coalition troops relied on the commands of Von Blücher and Wellington. The initial opening clashes of this campaign began on June 15th, as the French crossed the River Sambre near Charleroi, defeating the Prussian positions and securing a favorable position at the junction between the temporary encampments of Wellington's troops and the Prussian army to the east. On the next day, the Battle of Quatre Bras was led, with Michel Ney commanding the French. The battle was led at a strategic crossroads and was costly in casualties. While it was essentially an indecisive battle, it was nevertheless a strategic French victory, as Napoleon managed to prevent Wellington from reinforcing the Prussians who were engaged in the Battle of Ligny which occurred at the same time. The Battle of Ligny was another *massive* engagement, and a decisive French victory. Napoleon then placed his right wing under the command of Marshal Grouchy giving him the order to pursue the retreating Prussians, while he himself would take the left wing and the reserves in order to pursue Wellington's forces towards Brussels. On the night of June 17th, Wellington learned that the Prussian army retreated from the Battle of Ligny mostly intact, and would be able to reinforce him. Thus, Wellington turned his forces and prepared for battle on a gentle slope, near the village of Waterloo. The next day would usher in the start of one of the most important battles of the entire Napoleonic Wars, and one that would remain etched in the pages of history.

The Battle of Waterloo lasted just a single day, but was a vicious and complex affair. The British managed to hold their ground against repeated and ruthless French attacks. However, the Prussians began arriving as relief in the late afternoon in successive waves, attacking Napoleon's flank and inflicting heavy casualties on him. At the same time as the Battle of Waterloo was underway, Marshal Grouchy - whom Napoleon had sent in pursuit before - was leading the Battle of Wavre against the Prussian rearguard. This was a blocking engagement by the Prussians, which effectively kept Grouchy and his 33,000 men from aiding Napoleon at Waterloo. In the end, after suffering heavy casualties, Napoleon lost at Waterloo, and began a chaotic retreat back towards Paris. The British and the Prussians were hot on his heels, pursuing the French to Paris. Napoleon arrived there before them, and hoped to secure political support for further operations. He was still adamantly driven by hope that he could remain in the fight, even after losing 41,000 men just a few days before that at Waterloo. Napoleon hoped that he could organize a collective national resistance against his enemies, but this was far from reality. However, all of these hopes failed and he was eventually forced to resign - for good. Near the end Napoleon finally did something he never did before - he "laid down his sword" and finally admitted that he was defeated. When his brother Lucien Bonaparte, one of his last true allies, pressed him to "dare" as he used to dare before, Napoleon replied: "*Alas, I have dared only too much already*". Napoleon Bonaparte, that zealous leader that brought the biggest powers of Europe to their knees, had lost his fight. He abdicated in favour of his son on June 22nd, 1815.

Following the abdication, Napoleon received word that he must leave Paris. The Prussians who were encroaching had orders to capture him either dead or alive. Napoleon thus first fled to Chateau Malmaison outside Paris, and from there to the port of Rochefort. From there he hoped to be able to reach America. However, the Royal Navy in blockade prevented his goals from coming to fruition. In the end, being unable to either leave France or stay in it, Napoleon surrendered to the captain of the British ship HMS *Bellerophon*, which took him to England. From there, Napoleon was eventually exiled to Saint Helena, a highly remote island lying some 1,950 kilometres (1,210 mi) west of the coast of southwestern Africa. Napoleon remained there in exile, writing his memoirs in general isolation. He died there on May 5th, 1821. He was 51 years old.

Napoleon desired to be buried at the banks of the river Seine. However, if this was not to be allowed, he desired to be buried on Saint Helena, as he said: "*Have me buried in the shade of the willows where I used to rest on the way to see you at Hutt's Gate, near the fountain where they go to fetch my water every day*". This was referring to English East India Company's doctor, Mr. Kay, whom Napoleon often went to see after his long walks amongst the many flowering geranium bushes. In fact Napoleon himself called the valley *Vallée du Géranium* (Geranium

Valley). He was buried there, in the shade of a solitary willow tree in a simple tomb with a slab that was left completely blank. Only later, in 1840, his remains were exhumed and he was buried in an elaborate, majestic crypt beneath the Les Invalides dome in Paris, where his remains rest to this day.

Chapter XI
The Napoleonic Era Battlefield

THERE ARE A LOT OF factors that make the Napoleonic Era warfare so much different from some of the other historical periods you might have read about. This was not the age of the fast paced, chaotic, and modernized warfare of the 20th century - this was the era of gunpowder, of maneuvers, of line battles and grand, masterful strategy. In many ways, the Napoleonic Wars served to teach all the generals and commanders that would emerge in decades and centuries after about the "art" of strategic warfare. Some of Napoleon's greatest battles would be studied in immense detail, dissecting his tactical genius in order to draw out great lessons for the future battles. However, his approaches to battles could not be always utilized, and it became clear that - with the rapid modernization of the early 20th century - the old style of warfare was quickly becoming obsolete. A critical example is the Great War, in which the old clashed with the new, and at a huge loss of life. Nevertheless, in his era, Napoleon was unprecedented as a leader and a commander. He boasted a charisma that his generals and Marshals, as well as his soldiers, grew to love. That charisma he transferred even onto the battlefield. He was likewise a master strategist, bringing tactical innovations to the field of battle, without fearing to dare and take risks. Often enough, numerical disadvantage was no issue for Napoleon - in fact, he won some of his crucial battles while severely outnumbered. During the French Revolutionary Wars, and his early military career, he honed his skills as a leader of men, and gradually learned to combine new, modern (for the time) military tactics, with old and proven army formations. This approach developed into a flexible and very adaptive strategy, which would come to define some of his later battles. Napoleon's masterful grasp of grand military strategy is certainly what gave him some of his finest victories: he thought in advance and always knew when and how to exploit a sudden enemy weakness.

It was all this that gave Napoleon a clear upper hand over his enemies, many of which were still relying on aging and established strategies of much simpler warfare. And it was Napoleon who showed them that this simplicity simply is not enough. For his enemies, warfare was still much too crude - and often enough it all boiled down to simply outflanking your enemy. Before the Napoleonic Wars, entire armies would often surrender whenever they were outflanked. But by the time Napoleon came, this focus on flanking brought with it a whole set of flaws - commanders would work so hard to secure their flanks, that they would weaken their center and rearguard. Thus, he quickly learned to exploit this aged strategy, adapting to the enemy's style of battle and breaking the norms of warfare. Some of his iconic moves would win him the famous Battle of Austerlitz, such as the feigned flank attacks, or deliberate weakening of his own flanks as bait. In combination with this, he would utilize his strong and fearsome cavalry, with which he'd break the enemy's weakened center and envelop their split flanks to secure a victory. Lastly, throughout the Napoleonic wars, as we often touched upon, Napoleon would keep his most elite troops - the Imperial Guard - at his beck and call, relying on their vicious expertise to "cement" a victory or turn the tide of a fluctuating battle.

As part of the successful command over a battlefield, the commander of the Napoleonic Era had to rely on an efficient combination of infantry, cavalry, and artillery, but also on a variety of complex tactical formations. Often enough, it was the formation that was utilized that dictated the fate of a unit on the field. So, for example, the *attack* **column** was one of the widely used and highly efficient formations that Napoleon relied on. Known as the *colonne d'attaque* by the French, this formation was almost a hybrid of a column and a line. Napoleon utilized it as a continuation of the early "mob tactics" of the *Levée en masse* armies of the French Revolutionary Wars. The attack column relied on light infantry skirmishes, combining devastating musket salvoes and bayonet charges. While excellent against a standard line of skirmishers - which it would often break with certainty - this massed formation was vulnerable to cannon fire. The **square** was equally important as a formation, and could greatly prolong the lifespan of a unit on the field. The French knew it as *carré,* and as a versatile defence against cavalry. Strongly reminiscent of the ancient roman *testudo,* the soldiers would form a hollow square, with each side being at least three ranks "thick". Such a square was protected on all sides from charges and cavalry. Nevertheless it was largely a stationary formation, and thus vulnerable to focused artillery fire.

But when it came to breaking enemy morale and devastating a line formation, there was no better solution than the **wedge**. This iconic cavalry formation, called the *colonne de charge* in French, was shaped as a spearhead, and utilized to quickly form up and devastate a stationary line with speed and cold steel. However, it was not supposed to lose the momentum once it was gained - if a cavalry charge was stopped, it became very vulnerable. The so-called *Tête du sanglier* - the **boar's head** formation was also often utilized. As a very complex, hybrid formation, it utilized infantry, cavalry, *and* artillery all at once in a mixed order that resembled - as the name suggests - the head of a wild boar. Very difficult to set up, it was nevertheless very effective as an offensive formation, albeit slow moving.

During the course of the Napoleonic Era, artillery played a highly important role on the battlefield - perhaps even crucial. Napoleon himself was trained as an artillery officer, and has famously stated that *"God fights on the side with the best artillery".* And just as the devastation of artillery fire would play the crucial role in the Great War, so it did dominate the Napoleonic battlefield. For the French Great Army, it was its backbone - the thundering hammer that pummeled the enemy lines. Their success relied on the ability to inflict mass casualties in the shortest amount of time. With a variety of shell types available at the time, an experienced artillery unit could adapt to several combat conditions - with varied results. One of the revolutionary methods that Napoleon devised was the highly mobile infantry. With excellent training that his crews got, they could swiftly relocate to a more suitable position, often accompanying infantry and reinforcing weakened positions and breaking enemy lines. But, most importantly however, the French artillery was more advanced than that of their enemies. The French cannon design was greatly modernized in mid 1700's by Lieutenant General Gribeauval, whose design allowed for lighter, more efficient, and easier to produce guns, without any sacrifice to range or firepower. And it was his design that would be crucial for French artillery's success. Napoleon made it even better by managing to devise a tactic that would easily integrate his cannons with cavalry or infantry units, creating a sort of hybrid with great success. However, they would still be able to operate independently and from range. The *foot artillery* was designed as to travel at the pace of infantry. When not deployed, they were drawn by horses and the gunners marched beside the gun. It is interesting to note that an artillery battery included much more than just the crews and their officers. There were also drummers, wood and metal workers, trumpeters, fur workers, and other artisans - all of which were critical for the effective work of a cannon.

However, the lighter cannons were reserved for the *horse artillery*. These fast moving, flexible mounted artillerymen were designed to support the cavalry, as a sort of hybrid between the two. With their fast firing, fast moving cannons, they could be deployed very fast at the desired position, but could also retreat at a moment's notice. With extensive training, these crews could achieve record time of deployment, where they would deliver a devastating barrage on the enemy lines, and equally quickly "pack up" and redeploy elsewhere. Note that the elite horse artillery units of the Imperial Guard were highly skilled. It was proven that they could go from riding at full gallop to firing their first shot in under 60 seconds! This was an incredible achievement under any circumstances, and the Duke of Wellington was astounded after witnessing such performance in battle. But, this effectiveness came at a steep price - literally. They were very expensive to raise and maintain, and thus were very few in number. All artillery units - foot and horse - relied on a variety of shells, but the most common one used was the classic, cast iron round shot. Very deadly at speed, it was also dangerous when losing momentum at long ranges, even though it bounced on the ground. But at close range it would cause carnage and devastation, tearing through flesh. However, they were quite inaccurate, especially at long range.

But one cannot talk of the Napoleonic era battlefield without focusing on the plain old infantryman. Theirs was the least glamorous calling - but it was what defined the core of the battle, and could dictate victory or defeat. The regular foot soldier bore the brunt of the carnage and work in the war. To be an infantryman in the Napoleonic wars, and to stand in line facing the enemy - was certainly a task reserved for those with courage aplenty. As line formations were dominant in the period, one had to almost "wait" and hope not to get shot. The muskets in use during this period were muzzle loaded weapons, and were reloaded with a process that entailed several crucial steps, like pouring gunpowder, the projectile, ramming it down, cocking the mechanism, and so forth. This made the rate of fire for a regular soldier roughly 3 shots per minute. What is more, these muskets were often inaccurate, and there was a common joke amongst the soldiers that in order to kill a man, one had to spend an amount of lead that equaled his own body weight. Most soldiers - both French and others - were required to complete a whole series of steps before being able to fire a single shot. These included: opening the priming pan; taking a pre-packed cartridge from his waist pack; biting off the tip of that packet; priming the musket by pouring a little bit of the powder inside the priming pan; closing the pan; pouring the remaining powder down the gun barrel; ramming the rest of the packet (which contained the projectile) inside the barrel; removing the ramming rod from its holder; ramming the contents into the barrel; returning the rod to its place; and finally making his shot. The process would then repeat all over. From this series of steps you can realize that it took considerable effort just to shoot a musket, and thus a soldier wanted to do anything to make his shot count. Nevertheless, with rigorous training and endless repetitions - and some "not-in-the-rules" shortcuts - the regular infantryman of the era could achieve a rate of fire of 3 to 4 shots per minute, and under the best of conditions, 6 shots was possible too. One of the most commonly found muskets on a Napoleonic battlefield, and also one of the favorites, was the French model 1777 *"Charleville"* musket. It was roughly 151.5 centimeters long, and also featured a fitting for a vicious 45.6 centimeter bayonet.

To paint an even dire picture of how harsh the life of an infantryman was, we must mention two facts. First, the general inaccuracy of the musket which was notorious. Even the veteran soldier during the Napoleonic Wars had to train regularly, some up to 3 times a week. One interesting experiment conducted during that period showed that out of an assembly of 720 French infantrymen, just 52 hit the target of 3 meters at a distance of 100 meters. When that distance was increased to 200 meters, there were only 18 hits. However, at a very close range, a salvo of shots fired from a line formation had devastating effects. That is why soldiers often waited until the last possible moment to fire their shots. The second factor we need to remember is the shot itself, and the effects it produced. When the trigger was pulled and the gunpowder was ignited, it produced a big, spark-filled flash. The shot also left a huge cloud of smoke. Once multiplied, this smoke clouded the field, and often obscured the view in front of the soldiers. And not only that, but it also gave a peculiar odor, reminiscent of a spoiled egg. So, the regular infantry man was often blinded, deafened, choked, and shaken by the repetitive shots of his own musket. And all the while, he had to repeat all the reloading steps, hoping that he won't die. The classic historian of the Napoleonic Era, John Elting, famously wrote that *"the enormous din and rattle of 500 muskets is completely beyond imagination"*.

Sadly, friendly fire was also a common occurrence in this period. This was often due to the complex and colour-filled uniforms of the soldiers, where at times it was difficult to distinguish an ally from an enemy. Add to this the smoke from your musket, and it can become rather confusing in the heat of battle. For example, at the Battle of Austerlitz, the combined effects of the dense fog and the massive clouds of gunpowder smoke completely blinded the soldiers on both sides. A notable example of friendly fire occurred in 1809, during the famed Battle of Wagram. The French soldiers mistook their allies, the Saxon soldiers, who were dressed in white uniforms, and opened fire on them. This was due to the fact that the Austrians also wore similar white uniforms. During the Battle of Waterloo, the Prussian troops thought that their allies of the Duchy of Nassau were Frenchmen due to their similar uniforms, and exchanged vicious fire with them for 10 minutes before the mistake was noticed. All of this tells us that life on the field of battle was very difficult when you were a common soldier.

Aftermath

THE EFFECTS THAT THE Napoleonic Wars had on Europe and the world were immense. Due to the sheer scope of this conflict, and the many nations it involved, it had lasting and widespread effects. In Europe, radical changes occurred during this conflict and in its aftermath. In his height, Napoleon managed to bring most of the Western Europe under his rule and under French dominance. However, what this meant was that his conquest of numerous territories brought with them the effects of the French revolution, in a time when much of Europe was still under the rule of monarchies. Napoleon brought with him democracy, court processes, abolition of serfdom, reduced power of the Church, and many more limits upon such relics of the Middle Ages. He also placed constitutional limits on the monarchs and nobles, and that was what made him so unpopular in those circles. However, even when Napoleon was defeated for the last time, those new freedoms and rights that he brought remained planted in the minds of many. And that served as a great wave that set many critical changes into motion, many of which shaped the world as we know it today. Napoleon's fierce economic war with Britain and his numerous trade restrictions served to showcase the importance of the artisans, of the middle class and the wage workers. With their voices being heard, and their importance at last made clear, the monarchs and the nobles that returned after Napoleon could no longer effectively assert their cruel, exploitational, and absolutist rule as they used to before, and that gave rise to more human rights. Even today we can rely on a reliable form of civil law with clear codes of law that are a legacy of the Napoleonic Code which he brought.

Nevertheless, with the war's end, the dominion of France in Europe came to an end. The major Coalition powers sat at the Congress of Vienna and tailored a new map of Europe that changed the national boundaries, all in hopes of creating a "balance of power" to ensure peace. Thus, after the Congress of Vienna, certain changes came into action. Prussia was finally made one of the "Great Powers", after being granted many territories, including parts of Saxony and Poland, and of Rhineland and Westphalia. After this improvement, Prussia became one of the industrial giants of the 19th century. Britain, arguably the least involved nation in the combat in Mainland Europe, emerged as the foremost economic power after the war. Of course, its Royal Navy retained its naval dominance of the global waters.

One important aspect that arose in the years following Napoleon is *nationalism*. With the Napoleonic Wars pitting the majority of European nations against one another, it awoke strong feelings of patriotism and national identity. The gap between the French and the German peoples dramatically increased. Of course, as we all know, this was a critical factor that shaped the future European history. And it was this sudden rise of nationalism that would be critical in the development of the First World War. In the century after the Napoleonic Wars, Europe would almost completely change its map, with old nations disappearing, and new emerging. What is more, some of Napoleon's changes during his rule were the critical factors that led to the later unifications and formations of - most notably - Italy and Germany. His Confederation of the Rhine can easily be considered as a precursor to a unified Germany.

Of course we cannot neglect the immense effects that the Napoleonic Wars had on the events unfolding in North and South America. The War of 1812 is considered by many as another theater of the Napoleonic Wars, and was an important, but largely fruitless episode in the history of the United States and Canada. But in the South America, these effects were much more important. The tumult in Europe spilled over across the seas and caused a wave of uprisings in the Spanish controlled South America, which led to bloody wars of independence and the emergence of modern South American nations as we know them today. North America felt another effect of the Napoleonic Wars, and that was migration. The Congress of Vienna essentially allowed for greater waves of migrations to the United States, and roughly 30 million Europeans migrated there in about a century, between 1815 and 1915.

Casualties

SUCH A WIDESPREAD AND devastating conflict cannot pass without immense cost of life. The Napoleonic Wars were marked by grand battles, which often employed tens of thousands of men at one time. This, combined with the high rate of casualties and with subpar conditions in the field, led to very high numbers of people killed. Furthermore, it is important to note that the Napoleonic Era lacked many of the amenities of the later periods. Medicine was still in its infant stages, especially in the field. Battlefield surgery was as crude as could be, and wounded soldiers were often left where they fell, since the only efficient method of evacuating them was by horse drawn carts. Disease was rampant during this period, as was starvation, and both of these factors contributed greatly to the final death toll. However, we need to take into account that the conditions of the period did not always allow for accurate records of casualties, and a lot of it was left to guesswork and calculations. The Napoleonic Wars were rife with battles – and many of them left fields littered with bodies. Mass graves were not uncommon, and soldiers were often stripped of their uniforms before burial. This left little in terms of careful identification. More than often, the dead and the dying were left on the battlefields days after a battle. After the Battle of Waterloo, thousands of bodies were left in the heat of the sun, some of the men wounded. Major Frye noted after the battle that *the sight was too horrible to behold*. Body snatchers and pillagers were a common sight after every battle, where they would rummage amongst the bodies looting them for valuables. One great insight into the state of things during the era are the

"Waterloo teeth". These pillagers would find fresh corpses of young soldiers with a good set of teeth which they would pull out. These teeth were sold en-masse to dentists across Europe, especially in Britain, who would fashion them into functioning sets of false teeth for ordinary British citizens. It was not uncommon in the decades after the Napoleonic Wars for the elderly people in Europe to be wearing a set of false teeth that once belonged to some unknown young man who lost his life in the war.

The sheer number of lives lost had a great negative effect on all countries involved, and had significantly destabilized the demographics of certain nation. France for example, would never fully recover from the tolls exacted by this conflict. It is estimated that close to 3,000,000 French people – military and civilian combined – lost their lives during this period. In the years following the war, the French population was severely shaken, especially in regards to the male-to-female ratio. After the war there was only roughly 0.857 males per each woman. France lost its demographic superiority over Germany, Austria, and the United Kingdom, in just a matter of few years.

The total numbers, of all nations involved, are far greater. Various estimates exist, usually averaging around 5,000,000 total deaths, and somewhere close to 7,000,000. One has to consider the difficulties of accurate estimates due to the numerous reasons that we mentioned above, and the far reaching consequences of this conflict. So, for example, the civilian deaths caused by the Napoleonic Wars can never be accurately determined. The reasons could be numerous, ranging from disease, starvation, exposure, poverty, atrocities, or anything in between.

Nevertheless, human sacrifice can never be overlooked. As we here read and write about numbers and statistics, we need to rouse ourselves from this indifference and see the story from a different, critical angle. We need to awaken in us that long slumbering empathy and to immerse ourselves into the age of Napoleon. To feel and envision the strife and suffering that countless men and women had to endure in the whirlwinds of global conflict. For these are not fictional figures. These are our ancestors, our forebears that had to endure in order to ensure a free future for those that followed. And their sacrifice can never be simplified by numbers and simple statistics.

Conclusion

THE WILL OF THE GREAT leaders of the world is often enough unshakable. Some are loved, some despised, some right – others wrong. But can they be in the right when their goals and missions turn into war? Can their causes be just and positive when lives are lost in order to achieve them? This could be the question which we will always ask ourselves. We can spend days with heaps of books, trying to dissect the Napoleonic Wars in the minutest detail, but we will never be able to justify the great loss of life that it caused. Napoleon's fight had its fair share of positive and negative aspects, making his figure sort of dualistic: some admire him, others not so much. But whatever his fight was for, we always need to remember that at his back, thousands and thousands of young men and women died – laying their lives at his beck and call. *"Dare"* his brother Lucien implored him, *"Dare as you dared before".* But Napoleon Bonaparte perhaps realized in that very moment that his *daring* cost Europe so much – irretrievably. *"Alas, I have dared only too much already",* he responded, perhaps thinking that no more lives could be spent on his own account anymore. One must wonder about the depth and the complexity of such great minds – which Napoleon without a doubt was. Spending his final years in isolation on the dreamy tropical island of Saint Helena, Napoleon Bonaparte was left to face all the ghosts and demons that might have haunted him. And if they did, they were certainly numerous. Was it a personal sacrifice to knowingly lead so many men to their doom and live with that burden? Or was it simply the immensity of his ego that did not allow him to think much about it? These are the questions that lie with Napoleon beneath the elaborate marble crypt in Paris, and questions we will never have the answers to.

By Aleksa Vučković

References:

BENNET, G. 2004. *The Battle of Trafalgar.* Pen and Sword.

Brnardic, V. 2004. *Napoleon's Balkan Troops.* Osprey Publishing.

Fisher, T. 2013. *The Napoleonic Wars: The Empires Fight Back 1808-1812.* Routledge.

Freedman, J. 2016. *Strategic Inventions of the Napoleonic Wars.* Cavendish Square Publishing.

Kiley, K. 2015. *Artillery of the Napoleonic Wars Volume II: Artillery in Siege, Fortress and Navy 1792-1815.* Frontline Books.

Mace, M. and Grehan, J. 2013. *British Battles of the Napoleonic Wars, 1793-1806.* Pen and Sword.

Mace, M. and Grehan, J. 2013. *British Battles of the Napoleonic Wars, 1807-1815.* Pen and Sword.

Maude, F. 1911. *Napoleonic Campaigns.* Encyclopedia Britannica.

Maude, F. 1998. *The Jena Campaign, 1806.* Pen & Sword.

McGrigor, M. 2004. *Defiant and Dismasted at Trafalgar: The Life and Times of Admiral Sir William Hargood.* Pen and Sword.

Mikaberidze, A. 2020. *The Napoleonic Wars: A Global History.* Oxford University Press.

Muir, R. 2000. *Tactics and the Experience of Battle in the Age of Napoleon.* Yale University Press.

Paret, P. 2009. *The Cognitive Challenge of War: Prussia 1806.* Princeton University Press.

Rapport, M. 2013. *The Napoleonic Wars: A Very Short Introduction.* OUP Oxford.

Roberts, A. 2001. *Napoleon and Wellington: The Battle of Waterloo and the Great Commanders who Fought it.* Simon & Schuster.

Robinson, C. 1911. *Peninsular War.* Encyclopedia Britannica.

Schneid, F. 2012. *Napoleonic Wars.* Potomac Books.

Warner, O. 2003. *Nelson's Battles.* Pen and Sword.

Weider, B. and Franceschi, M. 2008. *Wars Against Napoleon: Debunking the Myth of Napoleonic Wars.* Savas Beatie.

Don't miss out!

Visit the website below and you can sign up to receive emails whenever History Nerds publishes a new book. There's no charge and no obligation.

https://books2read.com/r/B-A-ODOK-MWYKB

BOOKS 2 READ

Connecting independent readers to independent writers.

Also by History Nerds

Celtic History
Ireland

Great Wars of the World
World War 1
World War 2
The Napoleonic Wars: One Shot at Glory
The Serbian Revolution: 1804-1835
Peace Won by the Saber: The Crimean War, 1853-1856
The Wars of the Roses

Irish Heroes
Grace O'Malley: The Pirate Queen of Ireland
William Butler Yeats: Nobel Prize Winning Poet
Scáthach
Finn McCool

The History of the Vikings

Vikings
Longships on Restless Seas

The Rise and Fall of Empires
Rome: The Rise and Fall

Standalone
The History of the United Kingdom
The History of Ireland
The History of America
Stalin
The Fiery Maelstrom of Freedom
The History of Scotland
Robert the Bruce
William Wallace: Scotland's Great Freedom Fighter
The History of Wales